Applying Requirements and Business Analysis

Jean-Michel Bruel • Sophie Ebersold
Mariya Naumcheva

Applying Requirements and Business Analysis

Jean-Michel Bruel
Université Toulouse Jean Jaurès
Toulouse, France

Sophie Ebersold
Université Toulouse Jean Jaurès
Toulouse, France

Mariya Naumcheva
Université Toulouse Jean Jaurès
Toulouse, France

ISBN 978-3-031-92159-9   ISBN 978-3-031-92160-5 (eBook)
https://doi.org/10.1007/978-3-031-92160-5

© The Editor(s) (if applicable) and The Author(s), under exclusive license to Springer Nature Switzerland AG 2025

This work is subject to copyright. All rights are solely and exclusively licensed by the Publisher, whether the whole or part of the material is concerned, specifically the rights of translation, reprinting, reuse of illustrations, recitation, broadcasting, reproduction on microfilms or in any other physical way, and transmission or information storage and retrieval, electronic adaptation, computer software, or by similar or dissimilar methodology now known or hereafter developed.
The use of general descriptive names, registered names, trademarks, service marks, etc. in this publication does not imply, even in the absence of a specific statement, that such names are exempt from the relevant protective laws and regulations and therefore free for general use.
The publisher, the authors and the editors are safe to assume that the advice and information in this book are believed to be true and accurate at the date of publication. Neither the publisher nor the authors or the editors give a warranty, expressed or implied, with respect to the material contained herein or for any errors or omissions that may have been made. The publisher remains neutral with regard to jurisdictional claims in published maps and institutional affiliations.

This Springer imprint is published by the registered company Springer Nature Switzerland AG
The registered company address is: Gewerbestrasse 11, 6330 Cham, Switzerland

If disposing of this product, please recycle the paper.

Foreword

Engineers build solutions. Software engineers build *software* solutions: programs. The principal concern of software engineering as a discipline is to ensure that a program is of good quality. Who cares, though, if it is the solution to the wrong problem?

Enter requirements engineering (or business analysis), the part of software engineering that dedicates itself to analyzing the problem and ensuring that the solution addresses it. Its dubious distinction is that it is the subfield of the discipline that exhibits the biggest chasm between theory and practice. Theoretical advice on how to perform requirements abounds, supported by a considerable literature presenting numerous methods; they have had hardly a dent on most industry projects, which largely limit themselves to two fairly simplistic techniques, use cases and user stories. The state of software technology would improve significantly if we could reduce the gap and help industry perform better requirements.

My *Handbook of Requirements and Business Analysis*, first published in 2022, took a step in this direction by introducing a simple approach to requirements, closely integrated (in the spirit of "seamless development") with the rest of the software lifecycle, traditional or agile. It takes a comprehensive view of requirements, covering four aspects known as the "four PEGS": Project, Environment, Goals, System. It comes with a "Standard Plan" for requirements specification, with one "book" for each of the four PEGS, each with standard sections providing a checklist of the questions that an effective requirements process must ask and answer.

For brevity and focus, the Handbook focuses on analysis and principles, supported by a sprinkling of mostly short examples. Many of the people who read the book and want to apply or teach its approach have told me that they would also benefit from more detailed, hands-on examples and guidance. The present book makes that dream come true.

A group of researchers and educators in the SM@RT team at IRIT, the computer science institute of the Université Toulouse Jean Jaurès, has been using the PEGS approach for several years in research and teaching. To share some of their expertise and help software engineers produce successful requirements, Jean-Michel Bruel, Sophie Ebersold, and Mariya Naumcheva have put together this "Companion" volume.

The first chapters present a practical summary of the key concepts, in an operational, how-to style making them directly applicable by practitioners.

The most important chapter presents detailed requirements for several case studies. As warm-up, it starts with a library management system. The second example is a self-application of the approach: devising the requirements for a book project devoted (who would have guessed?) to practical requirements engineering. It is followed by the largest case study, which develops the requirements for a significant industrial application in a challenging area (cyberphysical systems); the target is a key part of Roborace, a system controlling self-driving Formula 1 cars.

Chapter 6 provides a thoughtful review of lessons learned. In line with its resolutely practical approach, the book also includes appendices with reference information: a glossary of requirements engineering terminology, a summary of rules and principles, categories of requirements and stakeholders, and standard requirements plan.

It is both gratifying and intimidating to see one's work taken up by others and extended in new directions. This book is not just a Companion but an important contribution of its own, which will be precious to anyone intent on applying proven requirements techniques as part of a quality-focused software process. I hope many practitioners will benefit from it.

Zurich, Switzerland   Bertrand Meyer

Preface

This book is a companion to **Bertrand Meyer's Handbook** (called **The Handbook** in the remaining of this book). It provides a practical view of how to use requirements effectively. It contains complete examples and is a practical material that complements **The Handbook**. It addresses several kinds of readers.

Professional Practitioners
For professional practitioners looking for practical materials and guidelines to help them apply good practices and principles to handle modern requirements and business analysis, this book provides several implementations of the important ideas from **The Handbook** and is concrete and directly usable, with professional templates for the book plan, principles and rules implementations, and a detailed list of possible stakeholders.

Students
This book will be of much help to students wanting to train and learn modern practices toward requirements engineering and business analysis, whether their curriculum is based on **The Handbook** or not, as it has been written to be as self-contained as possible.

Teachers and Trainers
Teachers and trainers looking for complete case studies to discuss with their students, as well as some exercise solutions, examples, and discussions around modern requirements and business analysis will find this book useful. Almost all the practical materials described in this handbook are available on the **companion website**.

Toulouse, France
Jean-Michel Bruel
Sophie Ebersold
Mariya Naumcheva

Disclaimer and Conventions

The links and references (**which appear like this**) will only be useful if the reader uses this material's electronic version on a computer (e.g., PDF).

Conventions for this book:

- When we write about "the system," we mean the system under consideration or development (often referenced by the SOI acronym—System Of Interest).
- This companion book satisfies a list of requirements (see Sect. 5.2) as an illustration of the PEGS approach. The chapters (and sometimes the sections) are then linked according to their satisfaction of/relation to these requirements.
- The footnotes are grouped at the end of their corresponding chapter.
- Repetition is a pedagogical tool. This companion book, being mainly targeting students and learners, will use repetitions.

Some pictograms are used to differentiate the notes that complement the main text. Here are the meanings of these pictograms:

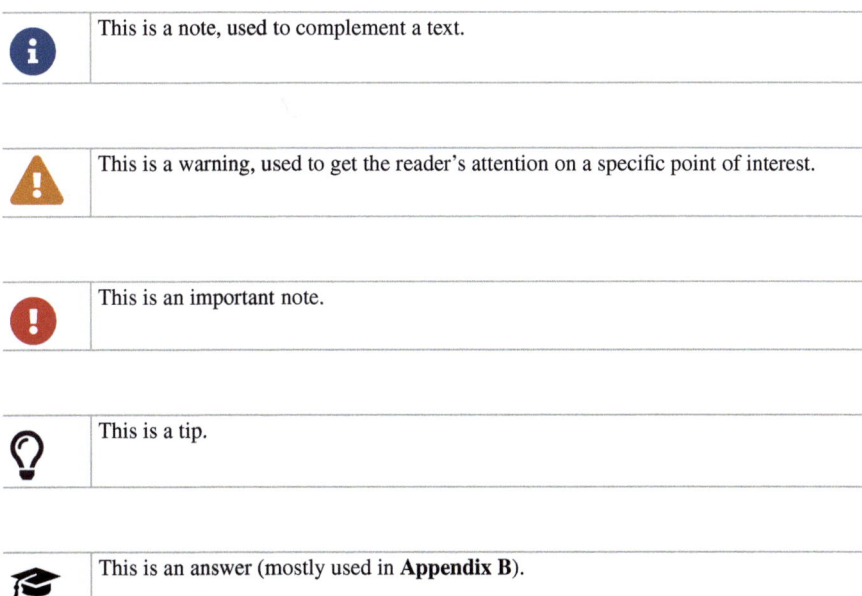

🛈	This is a note, used to complement a text.
⚠	This is a warning, used to get the reader's attention on a specific point of interest.
❗	This is an important note.
💡	This is a tip.
🎓	This is an answer (mostly used in **Appendix B**).

Acknowledgments

The authors are deeply grateful to Bertrand Meyer for the fruitful collaboration we have had during the past 10 years on requirements engineering. This collaboration has been an honor for us, and we are grateful for his patience and willingness to share, teach, and spread foundational principles in scientific research.

They would also like to thank all the people who have contributed to the material presented in this companion: their students (both PhD and MSc), Armando Fox for some ideas we have borrowed from his—*Engineering Software as a Service*—book, Sébastien Mosser for the ATCO EATS case study and the long discussions we had on teaching PEGS, Franck Silvestre for his review of the book, and finally all the colleagues, tutorial attendees, and friends who have provided feedback on the book and the **companion website** (including among others: Annie Meyer, Kim Gülle, Sungsoo Robert Ahn, Alessio Gambi, Michael Haufe, Ralph Paul, and many others we may have unintentionally overlooked).

And finally, we would like to thank our families for their support and patience during the writing of this book.

Contents

1	**Introduction**		1
	1.1	Why Read This Book	1
	1.2	A Guided Tour	2
		1.2.1 Principles and Good Practices Rules	2
		1.2.2 Requirements Kinds	4
		1.2.3 The Four PEGS	4
		1.2.4 Requirements Are Software	4
		1.2.5 Requirements Quality and Management	5
		1.2.6 Taking Advantage of a Formal OO Approach	7
		1.2.7 Life Cycle	7
	1.3	Organization of This Companion Book	8
2	**Presentation of the PEGS Approach**		11
	2.1	Basic Principles	12
		2.1.1 The Critical Role of Requirements Engineering	12
		2.1.2 Universe of Discourse	13
		2.1.3 Kind of Requirements	14
		2.1.4 How to Find the Category of Existing Requirements	24
		2.1.5 People Involved	25
	2.2	Standard Plan for Requirements	25
		2.2.1 The Four PEGS	25
		2.2.2 Metadata	26
		2.2.3 Goals	26
		2.2.4 Environment	31
		2.2.5 System	34
		2.2.6 Project	36
		2.2.7 Links Between the Four PEGS	40
	2.3	The Life Cycle Model	41
		2.3.1 The Definition Step	41
		2.3.2 The Implementation Step	41
	2.4	Frontier Between Requirements and Analysis	43
		2.4.1 Design Versus Requirements	43
		2.4.2 About Versioning and Variability	44
		2.4.3 What About Requirement Attributes?	44

3 Object-Oriented Requirements ... 47
3.1 Main Concepts ... 48
3.1.1 Class as the Core Concept of OO Requirements ... 48
3.1.2 Relations Between Classes ... 49
3.1.3 Contracts ... 49
3.2 Producing OO Requirements ... 52
3.2.1 How to Produce Object-Oriented Requirements ... 52
3.2.2 Eliciting and Documenting Requirements ... 53
3.2.3 Modeling Components of the System and Its Environment ... 53
3.2.4 Producing Functional Specification ... 54
3.2.5 Behavioral Specification ... 55
3.3 Requirements Traceability ... 57

4 Quality and Verification Criteria for Requirements ... 59
4.1 Books Mutual References ... 59
4.2 The "To Be Determined" Rule ... 61
4.3 The Minimum Requirements Outcome Principle ... 63
4.4 GitHub Implementation Example ... 63
4.5 Additional Guidelines for Quality ... 66

5 Case Studies ... 67
5.1 A Library Management System (LMS) ... 68
5.1.1 Context ... 68
5.1.2 Goals ... 69
5.1.3 Environment ... 72
5.1.4 System ... 75
5.1.5 Project ... 80
5.2 A Book on Requirements ... 82
5.2.1 Context ... 82
5.2.2 Changelog ... 82
5.2.3 Goals Book ... 83
5.2.4 Environment Book ... 86
5.2.5 Project Book ... 88
5.2.6 System Book ... 90
5.2.7 Traceability Matrix ... 91
5.3 The Roborace ... 92
5.3.1 Context ... 92
5.3.2 Goals Book ... 92
5.3.3 Environment ... 96
5.3.4 System ... 103
5.3.5 Project ... 107
5.4 Industrial and Other Use Cases ... 111

6	**Lessons Learned**		113
	6.1	Producing OO Requirements	114
	6.2	Concrete Use of a PEGS Book as an Initial Set of Requirements	115
	6.3	Requirements Engineering Course in Toulouse (2024)	115
		6.3.1 Active Learning	116
		6.3.2 Projects	116
		6.3.3 Outcomes	117
	6.4	Producing PEGS Requirements: A Study at the Constructor University	118
	6.5	McMaster University (2024)	119
		6.5.1 First Window of Opportunity	120
		6.5.2 Second Window of Opportunity	121
		6.5.3 Final Delivery	121
		6.5.4 Measurements	122
	6.6	PEGS Requirements for the MVP (2023)	123
	6.7	RE Conference Tutorials (2023 and 2024)	124

Appendix A: Glossary 125

Appendix B: Frequently Asked Questions 131

Appendix C: Categories of Stakeholder 141

Appendix D: Principles and Good Practice Rules 145

Appendix E: Book Templates 155

Appendix F: Exercises: Elements of Solutions 157

Appendix G: Handbook Errors in the First Edition (2022) 165

References and Links 167

About the Authors

Jean-Michel Bruel is a Full Professor and holds the Airbus Research Chair on Model-Based System Engineering at the University of Toulouse Jean Jaurès. His research areas include the development of software-intensive cyber-physical systems and methods/model/language integration, with a focus on requirements and model-based systems engineering. He has been teaching abstractions and modeling in various universities for almost 25 years.

Sophie Ebersold is a Full Professor at the University of Toulouse Jean Jaurès and Head of the SM@RT team at IRIT CNRS laboratory since September 2021. Her research areas are in software engineering and include the modelling of complex systems, which emphasizes methods/model/language integration and requirements engineering. She teaches various software engineering courses for bachelor and early master students.

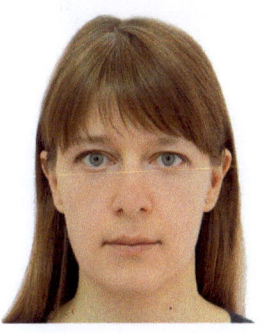

Mariya Naumcheva has a PhD from the University of Toulouse Jean Jaurès. Her main research area is requirements engineering, especially applying object-oriented techniques to requirements specification.

Introduction

1.1 Why Read This Book

This book is a companion and a complementary material to Bertrand Meyer's book, *Handbook of Requirements and Business Analysis* (referred to as **The Handbook** in the remaining parts of this book), published by the same publisher (Springer) in 2022. Its associated website is https://link.springer.com/book/10.1007/978-3-031-06739-6.

While **The Handbook** is general, most of its examples come from the software engineering domain. This companion book addresses a slightly broader spectrum by including examples from the systems engineering domain. It is a field where requirements engineering is an even more critical activity. (Who cares if your website crashes occasionally? Not so true for an airplane.) After all, as someone told us recently about **The Handbook**:

"I found your book quite valuable to bring normal software developer closer to the general ideas of structured, systematic system engineering and development."

—Ralph Paul, July 24, 2024

Whether you have already read or discovered **The Handbook, this companion book** will help you discover a new approach toward identifying and organizing requirements. You may use the PEGS approach in your business analysis class or your company to structure how this crucial step is conducted. In both cases, you will find in this **companion book** not only the principles of the PEGS approach but also a lot of illustrations, concrete cases, examples of implementation, practical advice, and materials to adopt the approach efficiently.

If we look at the place of the requirements in the overall development life cycle used by most organizations, they come first. Whether they are called requirements per se, user stories in agile methods, or use cases in UML-based approaches, one of the first steps is identifying the requirements related to the product, system, or software to be developed.

This requirements engineering phase is often split into different steps. For example, in the Wiegers & Beatty approach (see Wiegers 2013 for more details) they use three phases called business requirements, user requirements, and functional requirements. Each phase produces specific documents called *vision and scope document*, *user requirements document*, and *software requirements specification*.

In most industrial approaches we have studied, we can also define three phases, illustrated in Fig. 1.1: stakeholders requirements, system requirements, and system design requirements.

The PEGS approach, independent of the type and number of steps you split your requirements engineering phase into, focuses on organizing the requirements documents as efficiently as possible.

1.2 A Guided Tour

| If you have time for only one section of this book, this is the one! It aims at providing a complete overview of the PEGS approach and what makes it innovative.

As defined in **The Handbook**:

A **requirement** is a **relevant statement** about a **project**, **environment**, **goal**, or **system property**.
—Handbook, p.5

| The terms of this definition will be detailed in Chap. 2, "Presentation of the PEGS." *Approach*. Note that highlighted terms such as **statement** are defined in the Glossary (see **Appendix A,** *Glossary*).

The specificities of the PEGS approach are:

- To provide a set of well-defined principles
- To consider all the elements generally found in specification documentation as requirements
- To organize them in a systematic and structured way

1.2.1 Principles and Good Practices Rules

The PEGS approach is based on a set of principles, introduced linearly in **The Handbook**, when appropriate, and grouped in this **companion book** in **Appendix D**.

1.2 A Guided Tour

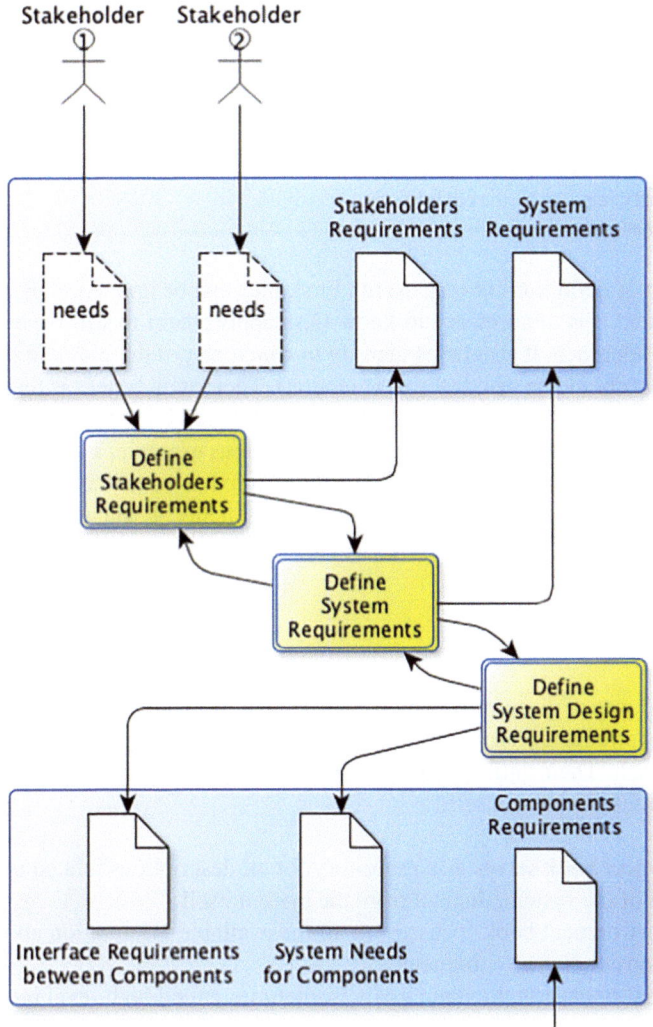

Fig. 1.1 Requirement engineering process (Adapted from MODRE 2016)

For example, the following principle summarizes the iterative feature of the PEGS approach, as well as the "just enough requirements" mindset that goes with it:

▤ **Requirements Evolution**
(See 2.1.4 of **The Handbook**.*)*

> Requirements are a living asset of any project, subject to evolution. They must be adapted and kept up to date throughout the project.

1.2.2 Requirements Kinds

As illustrated by Fig. 2.5, and detailed in Sect. 2.1.3, the PEGS approach proposes a set of well-defined categories of requirements. For example, a **constraint** is defined as:

> A **property** imposed by the **environment**.
> —Constraint

This set of definitions is very useful. First, they can be ignored; they are not prescriptive, and it is unnecessary to know (less apply) them to still benefit from the rest of the approach. It also helps identify in which part of the standard plan a given requirement should be listed (see next section). Their main benefit is that, if applied systematically, they allow for the definition of complex but important relationships between requirements. To continue with the previous example, a given organization might want to impose that any requirement identified as a constraint should be associated with the goal (another kind of requirement) it impacts (positively or negatively).

1.2.3 The Four PEGS

Four "universes of discourse," which complement each other, are proposed to organize the requirements. They are not just components but the pillars of a comprehensive approach. Their initials form the name of the approach: the four PEGS. Each will constitute a book in itself.

- The **P**roject book serves as a repository for all descriptions related to the development of the system, distinct from the system itself.
- The **E**nvironment book focusses on all the available information about the system's surrounding environment.
- The **G**oal book lists the main goals (sometimes called high-level requirements) from the stakeholders' perspective.
- The **S**ystem book lists the requirements of the system itself. It is then the closest document to the actual practices in requirements documents.

As illustrated by Fig. 1.2 and detailed in Sect. 2.2, each book is itself organized into well-defined chapters. Chapter **E1: Glossary**, for example, is where the important terms, acronyms, and domain-specific concepts will be defined.

1.2.4 Requirements Are Software

One of the principles mentioned in Sect. 1.2.1 is the **Requirements Nature Principle**, which states that:

📖 Requirements Nature
*(See 2.1.3 of **The Handbook**.)*

Requirements are software.

The PEGS approach takes advantage of the characteristics of the requirements that are shared with software (written by people, expressed in a notation, can be combined with other elements, subject to change, interacts with other elements, etc.) to also consider them as software artifacts. It allows us to apply the same benefits (versioning, verification, lean implementation, etc.), considering them as living assets, not just documents.

For example, we will detail in Sect. 4.4 that requirements can be stored and managed in a 🜉 **GitHub** repository. **Here** is an illustration of some label on the requirements, written as issues, according to the book they are part of.

 In 🜉 **GitHub**, one can choose colors for labels. Note how the labels in Fig. 1.3 respect the color convention from **The Handbook**.

1.2.5 Requirements Quality and Management

The Handbook provides a set of rules (e.g., its section 3.7 lists 11 style rules for expressing natural-language requirements) and principles, all listed in **Appendix D**. Their

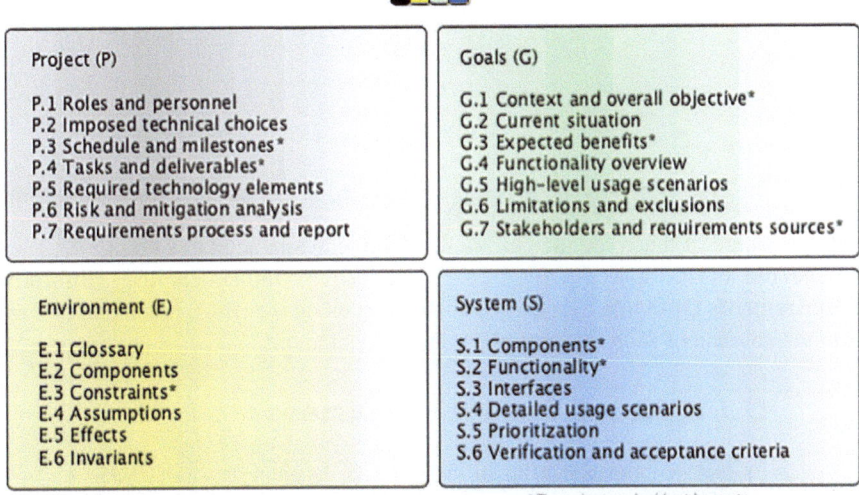

Fig. 1.2 The four PEGS (extract from the CheatSheet available at the **companion website**)

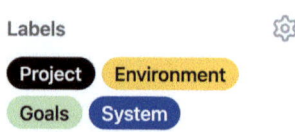

Fig. 1.3 PEGS as labels

precise definition allows them to be implemented according to the **environment** that supports requirements management. They will be detailed in Chap. 2, but here is an example and its concrete application.

One of the principles mentioned in Sect. 1.2.1 states that:

🗐 **Minimum Requirements Outcome**
(See 2.1.7 of **The Handbook.***)*

> The requirements effort must always produce the following elements.
> For the Goals:
> - Key business objectives (**G.1**). …

In our **AsciiDoc** implementation of the standard plan (see **Appendix E**), each chapter contains a note recapping its purpose, and a standard (but parameterized) text is used for still-empty chapters.

Excerpt of our Asciidoc template

```
=== G.5 High-level usage scenarios
NOTE: Fundamental usage paths through the system (see
{Handbook}).
{emptysec}
```

It allows the kind of homogeneous output illustrated in Fig. 1.4. The following command is a kind of macro defined as "⚠ Nothing available at this point."

The use of the macro `{emptysec}` helped us implement the **Minimum Requirements Outcome** by a simple shell script using the `grep` command to confirm the absence of such macro in the non-empty chapters.

G.5 High-level usage scenarios

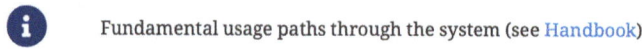

⚠ Nothing available at this point.

Fig. 1.4 PDF output of the `{emptysec}` command

1.2 A Guided Tour 7

 In addition to some external checking, it is always safe to remind the users of the standard plan, which chapter should not be empty. As such, we have added an explicit note in all our templates, as illustrated by Fig. 1.5.

1.2.6 Taking Advantage of a Formal OO Approach

The PEGS approach takes an innovative, object-oriented style of decomposition. Specifications are described and composed of units based on types of requirements. This style has proved its value in software development by yielding simple and clear architectures, facilitating change, and supporting reuse.

Figure 1.6 is an example of seven foundational classes and their relationships, using the Business Object Notation (**BON**[1]). The red arrows correspond to the inheritance relationship (Abstract Environment and Concrete Environment being two subclasses of the abstract class Environment). The blue arrows correspond to the usage relationship.

Some parts of requirements demand precision, at a level that can only be achieved through the use of mathematical methods and notations, also known as formal. When misunderstandings or ambiguities could cause the system to malfunction, the PEGS approach can help as a practical tool for formal requirements engineering. For example, the following is an excerpt of the formal definition of the **component** Sensor. It is represented as a (deferred[2]) class SENSOR (an abstraction of all the sensors).

```
deferred class
    SENSOR
feature
    position: LOCATION_3D
        --location in the world coordinates of the scene
    update_rate: REAL
        --sensor update rate
end
```

Extract of the Sensor.e class

Chapter 3 is entirely dedicated to an illustration of these benefits, taking advantage of the object-oriented method and Eiffel.

1.2.7 Life Cycle

The Handbook is not prescriptive about the method to follow for requirements engineering. For example, one can follow the process illustrated in Fig. 1.1

---

[1] See https://en.wikipedia.org/wiki/Business_Object_Notation.

[2] Meaning that is has no implementation yet.

G.1 Context and overall objectives

 High-level view of the project: organizational context and reason for building a system (see Handbook).

 This chapter should not be empty (following the *Minimum Requirements Outcome Principle*, p.27 of the Handbook).

Fig. 1.5 Little reminder

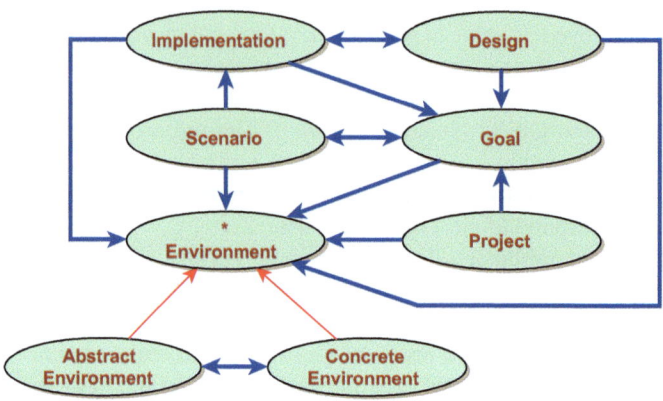

Fig. 1.6 Kinds of requirements as classes

[MODRE16]. Nevertheless, it provides a typical life cycle associated with the concepts of OO requirements described in the previous section. Those aspects are detailed in Sect. 2.3 (and illustrated in Fig. 2.25).

1.3 Organization of This Companion Book

This **companion book** has been developed following the approach advocated by **The Handbook**. Each chapter (and sometimes sections) can be considered as an artifact resulting from the development (or the consideration) of a certain requirement (or goal). Those requirements and goals are listed in Sect. 5.2. Vice versa, when pertinent, we indicate at the beginning of a chapter or section which particular requirement led to its development or consideration. Here is an example for the entire **companion book**:

▼ ⊘ *Corresponding Requirement*

> G.1.1 The main purpose of the **companion book** is to complement **The Handbook** by providing useful additional material, examples, templates, and full PEGS use cases.

1.3 Organization of This Companion Book

The remaining parts of this **companion book** will start with a detailed presentation of the PEGS approach in Chap. 2. Some of the specificities and subtleties of **The Handbook** will be explained and illustrated.

The following two chapters aim to demonstrate the benefits of the PEGS approach. Chapter 3 will detail the concrete use of the requirements, as defined and organized in the PEGS approach. Chapter 4 will illustrate some important quality rules that can be implemented in a concrete requirements analysis environment.

Chapter 5 covers in detail three concrete case studies using the PEGS approach: a classical information system (the Library Management System), the requirements we have defined to write this companion book (applying to ourselves our own recipe), and a real-life system (the Roborace).

Chapter 6 will conclude this **companion book** by listing some of the first lessons we have learned from applying the approach on industry, teaching materials, and student projects.

A set of **appendices** provides additional details and materials:

- A glossary of the important terms (**Appendix A**)
- A list of Frequently Asked Questions (**Appendix B**)
- A more detailed list of possible stakeholders (**Appendix C**)
- A comprehensive list of **The Handbook** rules (**Appendix D**)
- Some standard plan templates (**Appendix E**)
- Some exercises for teaching (**Appendix F**)
- Handbook errors in the 2022 edition (**Appendix G**)

Presentation of the PEGS Approach 2

▼ ⊘ *Corresponding Requirement*
This section satisfies requirement **S.1.1.1** (see Sect. 5.2).

Prerequisite
None! This chapter is an overview of PEGS. It aims to make this companion book self-contained by providing enough material to understand and use the main concepts and arguments. It does not require any previous knowledge of the method itself. Even knowledge about requirements engineering is not required for this chapter. For more details and a complete description of the subtleties of PEGS, we highly recommend referring to **The Handbook**.

What You Will Find in This Chapter
This overview chapter will cover the following material:

- A definition of requirements concepts and a classification of requirement kinds, in Sect. 2.1 (see **The Handbook**, chapter 1 for more details)
- A standard plan applicable to the requirements of any project, in Sect. 2.2 (see **The Handbook**, chapter 3 for more details)
- Precise guidelines on how to write effective requirements (see **The Handbook**, chapter 5 for more details)
- A presentation of the object-oriented approach to effective requirements (see **The Handbook**, chapter 8 for more details)
- How to make requirements a core part of the project life cycle (see **The Handbook**, chapter 12 for more details)

What You Will Not Find in This Chapter
This chapter does not cover the following aspects of PEGS that **The Handbook** fully addresses:

- General principles of requirements (see **The Handbook**, chapter 2)
- Quality criteria for requirements (see **The Handbook**, chapter 4)
- How to obtain requirements (see **The Handbook**, chapter 6)
- A discussion of the use case requirements technique (see **The Handbook**, chapter 7)
- An introduction to formal requirements, using mathematical rigor for precision (see **The Handbook**, chapter 9)
- An important kind of formal specification, abstract data types (see **The Handbook**, chapter 10)
- Completeness (see **The Handbook**, chapter 11)

2.1 Basic Principles

2.1.1 The Critical Role of Requirements Engineering

One of the biggest sources of software system quality problems is the failure to ask the right questions at the right time. The early phases of a project are particularly crucial in this regard. Studies have indicated that investing just 5% more effort in requirements engineering can potentially reduce overall costs by 30%.

There are numerous benefits to effective requirements management. Some of the key advantages are discussed below.

Improved Communication and Collaboration
Clear and well-defined requirements foster better communication and collaboration among **stakeholders**.

Defined Scope and Goals
A comprehensive set of requirements helps establish **project**'s scope and objectives, ensuring everyone is aligned with **project**'s vision.

Understanding Stakeholder Needs
Requirements-gathering processes help identify and understand the needs and expectations of all **stakeholders**, ensuring that the final **system** meets their requirements.

Risk Mitigation
Requirements management can help minimize potential risks and issues' impact on the project by identifying and addressing them early in the development process.

Prioritization and Direction
Well-defined requirements provide developers with a clear understanding of priorities and direction, enabling them to focus their efforts on the project's most critical aspects.

Traceability and Change Management
A robust requirements management process ensures that requirements can be traced throughout the development life cycle, making it easier to manage changes and maintain consistency.

2.1 Basic Principles

Quality Assurance and Validation
A solid foundation of requirements provides the basis for effective quality assurance, testing, and validation activities, ensuring that the final **system** meets the specified criteria.

2.1.2 Universe of Discourse

The PEGS approach considers and supports the trade-off between three forces pulling requirements in contradictory directions (see Fig. 2.1):

The Inductive Force
("Tell me what you want") that will focus on finding out what stakeholders really want (the stakeholders' wishes).

The Deductive Force
("Show me what you can do") that will help produce prototypes and demonstrations as early as possible in the life cycle (the product idea).

The Limiting Force
("No, you can't") that will bring both stakeholders and developers back to reality (the constraints).

PEGS takes its name (and **logo**) as a reminder of the four **dimensions** of requirements, leading to the organization of requirements in four books (Sect. 2.2 will detail this book's structure):

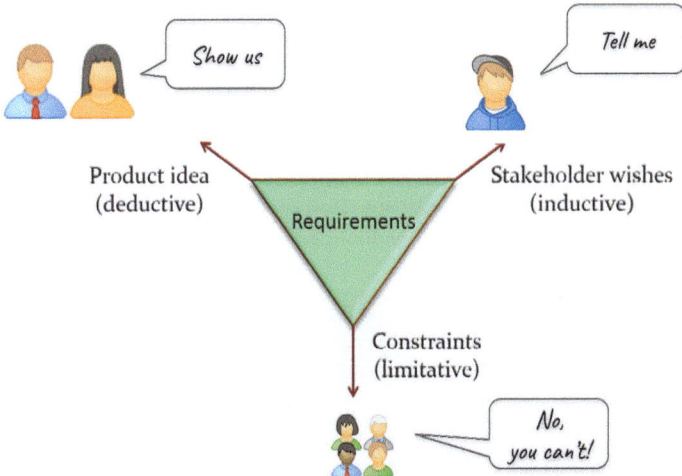

Fig. 2.1 Three forces pulling requirements

Fig. 2.2 The PEGS logo

Goals
the needs of the target organization, which the **system** will address

System
a set of related artifacts devised to help meet certain **goals**

Project
the set of human processes involved in the planning, construction, revision, and operation of the **system**

Environment
the set of entities external to the **project** and **system** but with the potential to affect the **goals, project,** or **system** or be affected by them

 All this book will follow, as much as possible, the color convention taken from **The Handbook,** and illustrated by the logo (see Fig. 2.2).

As we will illustrate in the remainder of this overview, this organization, while not mandatory, offers many benefits.

2.1.3 Kind of Requirements

As defined in **The Handbook**:

> A **requirement** is a relevant **statement** about a **property**.
> —Handbook, p. 5

We will illustrate graphically this definition by a blue bubble (the requirement itself) pointing at a white one (the **property** itself), as shown in Fig. 2.3. We will see in the upcoming concepts' definitions that this is a useful distinction.

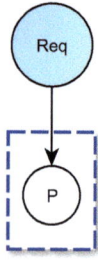

Fig. 2.3 A requirement is a relevant statement about a property

2.1 Basic Principles

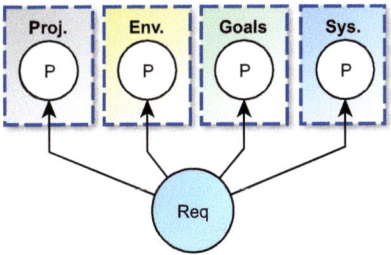

Fig. 2.4 A requirement is a relevant statement about a project, environment, goal, or system property

 This illustration convention is not used in **The Handbook**, but we find its pedagogical value worth mentioning here. It is also used throughout the slides provided in the **companion website**.

More precisely (see Fig. 2.4):

A **requirement** is a relevant **statement** about a project, environment, goal, or system **property**.

The term covers a wide range of possible statements; hence, **The Handbook**, introduces a set of kinds to organize and treat them accordingly.

 Some kinds have special cases (e.g., **role** being a special case of **responsibility**). Refer to section 1.3 of **The Handbook** for more details.

In the remaining subsections, we examine the 14 main kinds of requirements we have identified (and their special cases), listed in Fig. 2.5.

Some categories of requirements will only correspond to one of the four dimensions mentioned above (e.g., **goals**). Some will apply to all of them (e.g., **component**). Some will address a particular state of the system of interest (**SOI**), e.g., whether it is in development or running. We will then distinguish the different stages of a **system** (as illustrated in Fig. 2.6):

- The system itself (mainly to talk about its components)
- The running system (mainly to talk about its behavior)
- The system in development (mainly to talk about phases and artifacts)

Requirements Applying to All Dimensions

To describe the different kinds of requirements, let us start with the ones that may arise in all four PEGS dimensions: **component**, **responsibility**, **limit**, and **role**.

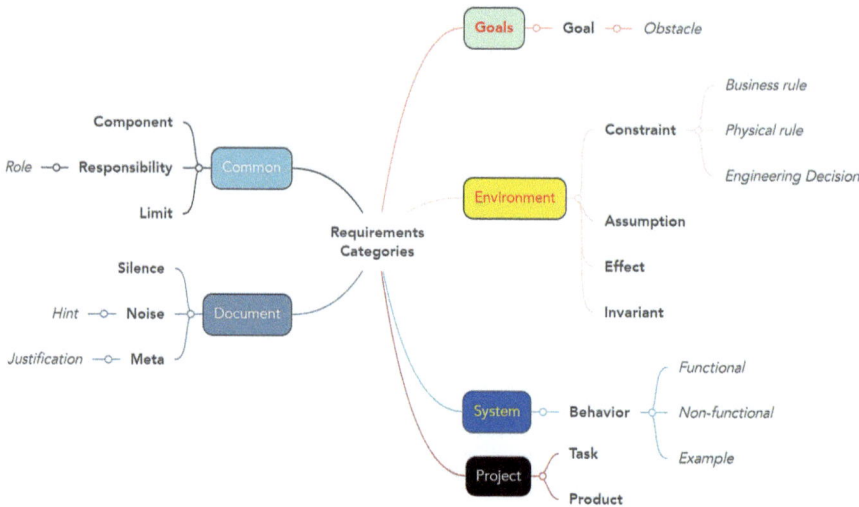

Fig. 2.5 The 14 main requirements kinds (and some of their sub-categories). https://requirements.university/

Fig. 2.6 Different stages of a system

Kind	Quick description
Component	Identification of a part (of a whole). See Fig. 2.7.
Responsibility	Assignment of **behavior** or task to component. See Fig. 2.8.

Kind	Quick description
Role (*special case of Responsibility*)	A human or organizational responsibility.
Limit	Exclusion from scope of requirements. See Fig. 2.9.

In a satellite environment, for example, the mention of an existing ground antenna is a **component** requirement that will belong to the Environment book. As **components** are expected in the Environment book (for external entities the system will interact with) and in the System book (for parts of the system), these two books have a dedicated chapter to list those **components** (respectively, **E.2—Components** and **S.1—Components**).

 It might be surprising to list components at the requirements level already. They could be considered as solutions (design decisions) rather than requirements. The reason is that systems are often not built out of the blue from scratch. They are built in an existing (sometimes very rich) context. S.1 and E.2 detail this context.

2.1 Basic Principles

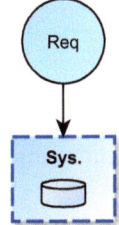

Fig. 2.7 Component: identification of a part

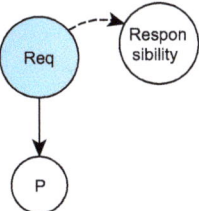

Fig. 2.8 Responsibility: assignment of behavior or task to component

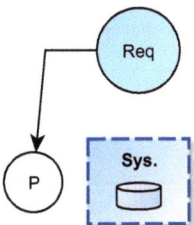

Fig. 2.9 Limit: exclusion from scope of requirements

Whenever a function, a task, a feature, or a **behavior** is explicitly allocated to a specific physical or human **component**, we will call this allocation a **responsibility** (or a **role** when dealing with humans).

Limits are helpful to precise the boundaries of the system (in terms of what are its concerns and what are outside). They will be mostly listed in the **G.6—Limitations and Exclusions** chapter. A Project book can mention some **Limits** regarding activities not addressed explicitly in the development project, for example.

| *Examples* |
| **Component** |
| "The Landing Gear System is composed of three parts: ..." |
| **Responsibility** |
| "The control system is in charge of the opening/closing of the door." |
| **Limit** |
| "The administration of the website is out of the scope of the system." |
| **Role** |
| "Authorizations are provided by the head of the audit department." |

You can find many more examples of these three kinds in all four dimensions of requirements.

Requirements Affecting Goals

The goal dimension is very specific to one kind of requirement: **goals**. Goals are concerns of the target organization, which the **system** must address. They are distinct from high-level functionalities. For example, the following statement is not a **goal**: "The goal of the system is to allow any user to book a flight." This one is a **goal** in our definition: "The goal of the system is to make sure as many users as possible book a flight through our app instead of the concurrent ones."

Using a Goal-Oriented Requirements Engineering (GORE) approach such as KAOS, you can organize them in some dependency graph and even define more specific kinds.

There exists one special case of **goal**: **Obstacle**. As they are similar to **goals** but defined negatively, it might be useful to tag them differently (e.g., to answer questions like "Have all the obstacles been addressed?").

> **Obstacle** in PEGS (a **property** to be overcome) has a different meaning than the one in KAOS (something prevents a goal).

Kind	Quick description
Goal	Desired result for the target organization. See Fig. 2.10.
Obstacle (*special case of* Goal)	Goal describing a **property** to be overcome.

> If you are surprised to see the term *Obstacle* but not the term *Rationale*, which often go together in other approaches (e.g., in SysML or KAOS), this is because, in **The Handbook**' classification, there is a special case of *Meta-requirement*, called *Justification* that plays this role.

> *Examples*
> **Goal**
>   "Current project focuses on developing autonomous driving software for Devbot 2.0."
> **Obstacle**
>   "The current manual operation of trains requires a minimum interval of 2 min between successive trains, preventing the tracks from operating at full capacity and making it impossible to meet the expected growth of traffic over the next 10 years."

Requirements About the Project

In the project dimension, the requirements address the project's specificities, such as **tasks** (e.g., design, testing, deployment) or **products** (e.g., test plans, libraries).

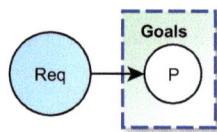

Fig. 2.10 A statement about a goal property

2.1 Basic Principles

A **task** describes the **property** that the project includes a certain activity. A **product** (sometimes called output, deliverable, or even artifact) is the result produced or the input needed by a **task**. They have a dedicated chapter in the Project book: chapter **P.4—Tasks and Deliverables**.

Kind	Quick description
Task	Activity included in project. See Fig. 2.11.
Product	Artifact needed or produced by a task.

In some domains, **tasks** can be defined as parts of activities and, in others, as a set of activities! It is important to understand the concept defined here as a *task* to align it with your organization's corresponding term.

Examples
Task
  "The team should meet daily; this meeting will be called a daily meeting."
Product
  "The following test plan is provided: …"

Requirements About the System

The following kinds of requirements relate to the "what a system must do" concern. They define some properties of the effects of the operation of the system or some of its components. They will be mostly found in the dedicated chapter in the System book: **S.2—Functionality**.

Kind	Quick description
Behavior	Property of the operation of the system. See Fig. 2.12.

Fig. 2.11 A task or a product

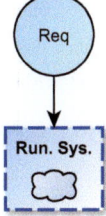

Fig. 2.12 A behavior is a property of the effects of some operation

Kind	Quick description
Functional requirement (*special case of Behavior*)	What the system must do.
Non-functional requirement (*special case of Behavior*)	How the system will perform.
Example (*special case of Behavior*)	Illustrative/representative scenario.

> *Examples*
> **Behavior**
> "The system should allow the user to open and close the door safely."
> **Functional requirement**
> - "The system should allow the user to open and close the door safely."
> - "Ability for Librarians to add and remove Books from the Library."
>
> **Non-functional requirement**
> "The response time of a window opening should be less than 0.1 s."
> **Example**
> "Here is the description of the use case `Cancel a previous order` ..."

Scenarios are a very popular way to express **behavior**. A **UML** Use Case, for example, is a very accessible modeling technique that does not require a strong background in modeling to read or even write. With the rise of agile methods, user stories are becoming another popular form of scenario definition. Let us mention another example of scenario description: test plans (or scripts).

Depending on the level of detail provided, scenarios can be found mostly in the Goals book (chapter **G.5—High-Level Usage Scenarios**) or in the System book (chapter **S.4—Detailed Usage Scenarios**).

> Make sure to link the scenarios in **G.5—High-Level Usage Scenarios** and the ones in **S.4—Detailed Usage Scenarios**.

Requirements About the Environment

A crucial part of describing the **system**'s expected **behavior** is the precise definition of its **environment**. These environment definitions, grouped in the Environment book, will characterize the conditions (e.g., nominal, exceptional) in which the **system** must behave.

Kind	Quick description
Constraint	Property imposed by environment. See Fig. 2.13.

Kind	Quick description
Business rule (*special case of Constraint*)	A constraint imposed by an organization.
Physical rule (*special case of Constraint*)	Consequence of the laws of nature.

2.1 Basic Principles

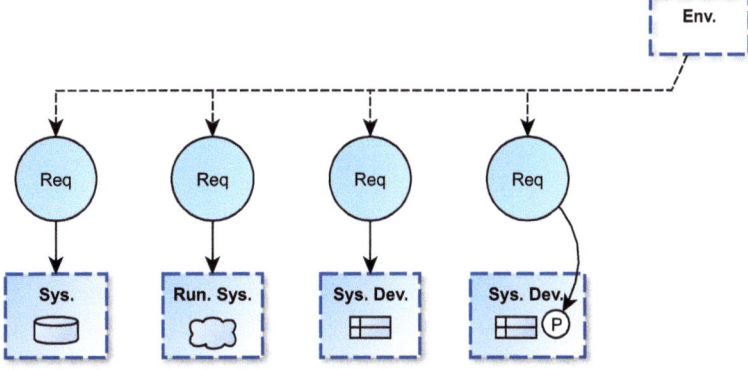

Fig. 2.13 Constraint: a property imposed by the environment

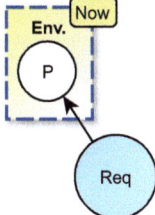

Fig. 2.14 Assumption: expected property of the environment

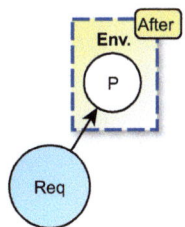

Fig. 2.15 Effect: property of the environment affected by the system

Kind	Quick description
Engineering decision (*special case of Constraint*)	Results from an explicit choice of the project.
Assumption	Expected **property** of the environment. See Fig. 2.14.
Effect	Property of the **environment** affected by the system. See Fig. 2.15.
Invariant	Environment **property** that must be maintained. See Fig. 2.16.

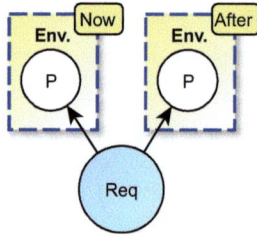

Fig. 2.16 Invariant: environment property that must be maintained

To be as precise as possible about the **environment**, it is important to list all the stakeholders and have them describe precisely their list of business or engineering rules. Most of the environmental requirements will be either **constraints** or **assumptions**. Section B.1.6 discusses the differences between a **constraint** and an **assumption**.

Examples
Business rule
"According to the regulation rule X.45F53, the amount of the engine CO_2 emission must be less than…"
Engineering decision
"According to our maximum reuse policy, our proprietary secured login system XYZ should be reused in this project."
Assumption
"The available bandwidth will be 1 Gbit/s or more."
Effect
"When the system is put into operation, employees will be paid on the last working day of the month."
Invariant
"The system expects a temperature between 18 and 25 °C (precondition) and maintains it in that range."

Document Description

In a requirements document, some parts are simply there to organize the **relevant** requirements (e.g., sections, legends, explanations). They might seem unimportant, but they are often very useful in understanding the requirements or their relationship with the stakeholders' **goals**. That is why they also need to be categorized.

An example of the importance of the relationship between a **meta-requirement**, such as a section's title and the list of requirements of that section, is that most of the time, those requirements are related. Sometimes, the section's title is a condition on the **environment** (e.g., "3.1 In park mode"), making all the following requirements under the same (non-explicit) **assumption** about the **environment**. It is easy to lose this **assumption** when translating one of the section 3.1 requirements into an effective system's function.

2.1 Basic Principles

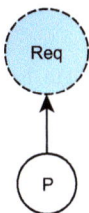

Fig. 2.17 Silence: property that is not in requirements but should be

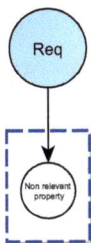

Fig. 2.18 Noise: property that is in requirements but should not be

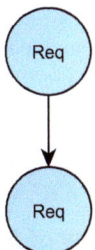

Fig. 2.19 Meta-requirement: property of requirements themselves

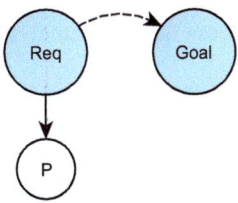

Fig. 2.20 Justification: explanation of a requirement

Kind	Quick description
Silence	Property that is not in requirements but should be. See Fig. 2.17.
Noise	Property that is in requirements but should not be. See Fig. 2.18.
Hint (*special case of Noise*)	Design or Implementation suggestion
Meta-requirement	Property of requirements themselves (not of project, environment, goals, or system). See Fig. 2.19.
Justification (*special case of Meta-requirement*)	Explanation of a project or system **property** in reference to a goal or **environment** property. See Fig. 2.20.

Examples
Silence
"The system should send the bill to the non-blacklisted customers." (How do we blacklist a customer? When do we send the bill, and how?)
Noise
"The director is not consistent in his decision-making."
Meta-requirement
"The details are provided in Fig. 2.1."
Justification
"The presence of two signature fields follows from the rule on purchases higher than € 5000 (section E.3.X)."

Where Are Your Types of Requirements?

In the above list, you should have found a corresponding kind for any of the ones you already use in your organization. For example, if you use the (ISO-29148)-*type* requirement attribute, you should have identified `Functional`, `Non-functional`, `Interface`, `Constraint`, or `Process` ones.

 There are some variations in the (ISO-29148) and the PEGS definitions for those terms.

What about the others? First, you can have a specific list of kinds, as long as you find it useful to help identify and manage these requirements. For example, the *ilities* (e.g., reliability, maintainability, security, etc.) in PEGS are included in the **non-functional** (sub-)kind.

2.1.4 How to Find the Category of Existing Requirements

In many cases, if you want to apply PEGS in your organization, you will start with existing sets of requirements.

Here is a systematic process we advocate to find their corresponding category:

1. Find the corresponding book between the four PEGS (see Sect. 2.2). This shortens the possibilities of categories.
2. Check if it is specific to this book or if it belongs to one of the three categories common to the four books (Component, Responsibility, Limit) or to the document categories (Meta, Silence, Noise).
3. Pick the best category in the remaining ones.

We also strongly advise you to read the frequently asked questions appendix (**Appendix B**). Feel free to contact the authors if you do not find answers to your questions. The FAQ list is aimed at growing with the most common ones.

2.1.5 People Involved

Requirements always involve humans, whether they were writing the requirements themselves, the documents the requirements were extracted from, or simply at the requirements' validation phase, which cannot avoid manual activity.

Each of the four PEGS books has its own set of people involved. The real person (while important in an organization for accountability purposes) is not particularly of interest here, but his *role* is.

Among the people involved with or concerned by the requirements, we can separate the ones that influence them, the **stakeholders** (e.g., company owners or engineers), and the ones who produce them, the **authors** (e.g., business analysts or subject-matter experts).

The Handbook provides a list of people involved. This **companion book** simply complements it with a checklist of categories of stakeholders (see **Appendix C**).

2.2 Standard Plan for Requirements

The proposed plan for requirements specification intends to simplify the (ISO-29148) standard and addresses the needs of modern projects.

The principles described in this chapter will remain, whatever tooling is associated with requirements management (database, spreadsheets, textual documentation, dedicated tools). Nevertheless, we should emphasize on the importance of configuration management in that context.

| Unlike the backlog-based approach advocated in agile approaches, our standard plan approach allows to decline, at each sub-system level, the requirements documentation (e.g., the System book at a system level becoming the source for the Environment book at a sub-system level). |

As illustrated by Fig. 1.2, requirements are organized into four main parts. These parts can become packages, folders, books, or databases. In the remaining description, we will consider dealing with a textual document such as Google Docs.

2.2.1 The Four PEGS

The organization of the requirements documentation in four books allows the authors of the requirements to focus on specific areas. There is no specific order in which they should write the requirements in terms of books (see a concrete example of steps in Fig. D.1). Nevertheless, we advise the authors to start with the Goals book, which provides the highest view of the system and focuses on high-level user goals.

While **The Handbook** does not prescribe a specific method for writing books, the case studies in this companion book have been written in a way that should not be considered prescriptive. This guided approach supports authors in determining system requirements while allowing flexibility to move between books as needed.

Below, we use the four PEGS books of a Library Management System to illustrate the purpose and usage of each chapter and section of the standard plan. The full version is available in Sect. 5.1 and can be downloaded at the **companion website**. In what follows, the Library Management System will also be referred to as the LMS (as stated in the metadata or in chapter **E.1—Glossary**; see Sect. 2.2.4).

```
Elements in this format will represent examples
extracted from the LMS case study in the following
sections.
```

 The requirements ID, links to references, etc. are generally omitted from the examples for readability purposes.

2.2.2 Metadata

Each organization might have specific additional information (explicit rules, disclaimers, legal notes, etc.). In PEGS, only front and back matters are used to illustrate such additional components.

Figure 2.21 illustrates the use of copyright information, disclaimers, and other organization notes.

2.2.3 Goals

The first book is the Goals book. By first, we mean "the first generally written." It deals with the needs of the stakeholders (mainly the target organization), which the system to be developed will address. It is composed of seven chapters.

Goals are the "needs of the target organization, which the system will address." While the development team is the principal user of the other books, the Goals book addresses a wider audience: essentially, all stakeholders.

It must contain enough information to provide (if read just by itself) a general sketch of the entire project. To this effect, chapter **G.3—Expected Benefits** presents

Control Information

Version	Delivery		Feedback	
	Deadline	*Delivered*	*Received*	*Integrated*
V1	15/08/2023	13/08/2023		
V2				
V3				

Disclaimer [1]

This document is provided for pedagogical use only, in the context of a requirements engineering courses delivered at McMaster University. **This is not a reference example of good requirements, as it deliberately contains flaws, errors and mistakes.**

This requirements document has been generated with the assistance of an AI language model. It is essential to acknowledge that while AI technology is a powerful tool, there are inherent limitations and potential flaws in using it to write requirements. As an AI language model, it operates based on patterns in data and past examples, which may not always capture the nuanced complexities of real-world scenarios.

The document may contain inaccuracies, ambiguities, or oversights due to the model's inability to comprehend context and intent as a human requirements engineer would. The AI-generated content might lack domain-specific knowledge, may not align with the latest industry practices, and could overlook critical requirements crucial for the success of the project.

Readers must exercise caution and critical thinking when interpreting the content. The requirements herein should be carefully reviewed, refined, and validated by experienced human requirements engineers and stakeholders with a comprehensive understanding of the project's context, objectives, and domain. The creators of the AI language model and this requirements document do not assume responsibility for any negative consequences arising from reliance solely on AI-generated content for critical decision-making in software development projects.

We will intensively use this document during the lectures to spot the mistakes that were made by the AI language model, and demonstrate the value requirements engineers adds to a project.

---

[1] This disclaimer has been entirely generated by ChatGPT

Fig. 2.21 Example of front matter (from **McMaster University** ATCO EATS case study)

a short overview of the system, and **G.1—Context and Overall Objectives** will typically include some key properties of the environment. As it addresses a wide readership, it should be clear and minimize the use of specialized technical terms. Together, **G.1—Context and Overall Objectives, G.2—Current Situation,** and **G.3—Expected Benefits** describe the rationale for the project. It is important to state these justifications explicitly. Typically, they are well understood at the start of the project, but management and priorities can change.

It can be difficult to identify if a requirement goes into the Goals or System books (later detailed). Our advice is to consider who the author of the requirement is or who is accountable for it. In the Goals book, the requirements are expressed from the point of view of the target organization. Requirements in the Goals book can be linked to "owners" who can validate them. These "owners" are typically individuals who are well-versed in domain/business-specific terms, which is why they are best suited for this validation process. This might not be the case with the requirements in the System book, which are written and verifiable by the people who will build the system itself.

G.1 Context and Overall Objectives

This chapter should not be empty (following the *Minimum Requirements Outcome Principle*).

```
The Library Management System can be used by any
existing or new library to manage its books, book
insertion, borrowing, and monitoring.
```

The first chapter of the Goals book is a general introduction that explains why the project is needed, recalls the business context, and presents the general business objectives. It provides a high-level view of the project: organizational context and reason for building a system.

"We want a Library Management System" is not a business objective and must not appear in this chapter.

Goals can also include non-functional needs such as:

```
The LMS is running 24 h a day.
Access to the LMS must be secured.
```

In the full version of the case study, nine general objectives have been formulated in the LMS specification.

The justification of the goals (rationale) is crucial and will be enforced by **G.3—Expected Benefits**.

G.2 Current Situation

> The Library Management System is described in this project, starting from scratch, based on manual library management and various public resources such as this one [...]

This chapter describes the current situation (if any) and justifies further why the project is needed. This allows the authors of the requirements to relate the system of interest with its **environment** (context).

G.3 Expected Benefits

 This chapter should not be empty (following the *Minimum Requirements Outcome Principle*).

> One of the six expected benefits of the LMS is "The system should enable its users to access basic library functions remotely, 24 h a day, according to their role in the system."

This chapter describes the business benefits expected from the successful execution of the project. This chapter is the core of the Goals book, describing what the organization expects from the system. It lists the new processes or improvements to existing processes made possible by the project's results.

G.4 Functionality Overview

> Patrons should be able to remotely consult the library catalog, put books on hold, know the remaining time for borrowing, and update their personal information.

This chapter provides a short overview of the future system, enabling the reader to grasp its concept quickly. It lists the main functionalities the system under specification must provide to its users and also says what users cannot do.

 The chapter only focuses on principal properties. Details will be found in the System book.

An example of a requirement expressing what LMS users cannot do is:

```
Patrons cannot update their borrowing information.
```

G.5 High-Level Usage Scenarios

```
All users must authenticate themselves before using
   the system.
Each user must have his or her correct username and
   password to enter into his or her online account
   and do actions.
```

This chapter provides the main scenarios (often in the form of use cases) the system should cover, which are depicted here. It lists the fundamental usage paths through the system.

 The scenarios chosen for appearing here should be limited to the main usage patterns and expressed in user terms, independently of the system's structure. The detailed usage scenarios will appear in the System book (more precisely in chapter **S.4— Detailed Usage Scenarios**; see **S.4**).

G.6 Limitations and Exclusions

```
The LMS does not manage support functionalities such
   as Web site management or HR management. This is
   expressed in this chapter by the following
   requirements:
The LMS only deals with book management and does not
   cover human resources management.
```

```
The LMS is not supposed to handle accessibility-
   related aspects. This is specified by:
Accessibility issues are not considered by the LMS.
```

This chapter specifies what the **system** will not do or does not need to address. This definition by negation is useful to precise the boundaries of the **system**'s responsibility.

G.7 Stakeholders and Requirements Sources

 This chapter should not be empty (following the *Minimum Requirements Outcome Principle*).

```
The LMS has the two following stakeholders […]
```

This chapter lists the **stakeholders** (groups of people who can affect or be affected by the project), other places to consider for information about the project and the system, and other requirements sources.

Stakeholders should be categories of people rather than individuals (e.g., "company CEO" rather than the person's name). To avoid forgetting any category of people whose input is **relevant** to the project, you should start from the detailed lists in "Categories of stakeholders" (see **Appendix C**).

2.2.4 Environment

The Environment book describes the application domain and external context, physical or virtual (or a mix), in which the system will operate. It is composed of six chapters.

E.1 Glossary

```
The glossary of the Library Management System will
  define LMS (the acronym used instead of Library
  Management System) as:
LMS: Acronym for Library Management System, the sys-
  tem under study in this case study
It defines also, for example:
Book: Copy of a book with a copy number and an avail-
  ability status
Library: Has a collection of Books and members that
  are patrons and librarians
Terms that are not system entities but non-func-
  tional elements or constraints are also defined:
Borrowing Period: Period during which a book can be
  borrowed
```

The glossary section provides clear and precise definitions of all the vocabularies specific to the application domain, including technical terms, words from ordinary language used in a special meaning, and acronyms.

Following the **Acronym Principle**, every acronym in the glossary should be explained (not simply expanded).

In terms of process, this chapter should be completed every time an important term is used in a requirement. By doing it systematically and regularly, the authors of the requirements will avoid having a dedicated time for this chapter.

It can be surprising that this chapter is not listed in the **Minimum Requirements Outcome Principle**. It comes from the fact that the requirements might only refer to general terms that do not need yet to be defined in the glossary.

 In some organizations, the glossary might be a separate document. Simply refer to it in this chapter.

E.2 Components

```
The LMS is interfaced with a Login Management compo-
   nent, whose development is under the scope of
   the system.
This is described by environment requirements such as:
The Login Management component would handle the login
   of the users (patrons and librarians) and their
   authentication.
The Login Management component is not dedicated to a
   library and can be an external module added to
   the LMS.
```

This chapter lists the elements of the environment that may affect or be affected by the system and project. It includes other systems to which the system must be interfaced.

 The **environment** elements that are process/development specific should not be listed here but in chapter **P.5—Required Technology Elements**.

E.3 Constraints

 This chapter should not be empty (following the *Minimum Requirements Outcome Principle*).

```
Twenty-two constraints have been written in the LMS
   Environment book, such as:
A book on hold is unavailable until the hold duration
   has expired or until the patron who placed it on
   hold has canceled it.
When the hold period expires, the book becomes
   available.
A patron is limited to five holds at any moment.
Hold duration is a maximum of 120 h.
```

This chapter specifies obligations and **Limits** imposed on the **project** and **system** by the **environment**. It describes all the important business rules, physical laws, or engineering decisions that the development will have to take into account.

E.4 Assumptions

```
The users can read French.
The users are assumed to have basic knowledge of com-
   puters and Internet browsing.
```

Assumptions are **properties** of the **environment** that may be assumed, to facilitate the **project** and simplify the **system**. It is not always easy to distinguish between an **assumption** and a **constraint**. We dedicate a section about that question (see **Section B.1.6**).

E.5 Effects

Effects are elements and **properties** of the **environment** that the **system** will affect. While the two previous categories concerned the influence of the Environment on the System, this one deals with the influence of the **system** on the **environment**.

```
The LMS will regularly update the Mayor House dash-
board to highlight citizen activities.
```

E.6 Invariants

```
The status of a book is available, on hold, borrowed,
due, or returned.
```

This section gives properties of the **environment** that the **system's** operation must preserve. The properties are assumed true before a **system** action and should remain true afterward.

2.2.5 System

The System book refines the Goals book by focusing on more detailed requirements about the **system** under development (or **SOI**), mainly its constituents, behaviors, and properties. It is composed of six chapters.

S.1 Components

 This chapter should not be empty (following the *Minimum Requirements Outcome Principle*).

```
The   LMS   has   four   components:   Books  Management,
   Patrons Management, Holds Management, and Checkouts
   Management.
Each of them is specified by requirements such as:
   - The  Books  Management  component  concerns  the
     books and includes books description.
   - The Books Management includes catalog generation
     with the  number  of  copies  available  for  each
     book,  searching  for  books  and  displaying  the
     list of books.
   - The   Patrons   Management   component   includes
     patrons'  identification  and  description,  with
     their first name, family name, ID number, address,
     and penalties.
   - The  Holds  Management  component  would  handle
     the holds.
   - The Checkouts Management component would handle
     the checking out and returning of books.
```

This chapter describes the overall structure expressed by the list of major software and, if applicable, hardware parts. It can be seen as the place to express the

2.2 Standard Plan for Requirements

Product Breakdown Structure (PBS), that decomposes the system into its constituent parts in the form of a hierarchical structure.

S.2 Functionality

 This chapter should not be empty (following the *Minimum Requirements Outcome Principle*).

```
A functional requirement in S.2.1 (Books Management)
is the ability for librarians to add and remove books
from the library.
```

This chapter contains a section, S.2.n, for each of the **components** identified in **S.1—Components**. A section S.2.n describes the corresponding behaviors (functional or non-functional properties).

S.3 Interfaces

```
Users should be able to access LMS from any device
that has Internet-browsing capabilities and an
Internet connection.
```

This chapter shows how the system makes the functionalities of **S.2—Functionality** available to the rest of the world. It lists user interfaces and program interfaces (APIs) handling the functionality and making them available.

S.4 Detailed Usage Scenarios

```
Reserve_a_book is one of the LMS scenarios: it is
   depicted as follows.
```

Detailed usage scenarios are examples of interaction between the **environment** (or human users) and the system: use cases and/or user stories.

 There should be a S.4.n section for each of the identified in **S.2—Functionality**.

```
Note that the Reserve_a_book scenario takes into
   account the E.3. constraint:
A patron is limited to ten holds at any given moment.
```

S.5 Prioritization

This chapter classifies the behaviors, interfaces, and scenarios (resp., **S.2—Functionality**, **S.3—Interfaces**, and **S.4—Detailed Usage Scenarios**) by their degree of criticality. This can be compared with the agile backlog, where user stories are tagged with priorities (often based on **MoSCoW**).

```
In the LMS, "Ability for librarians to add and remove
books from the library" can be considered the most
important functionality to manage, with "Reserve-a-
book" coming second in its nominal instantiation.
```

S.6 Verification and Acceptance Criteria

This chapter specifies the conditions under which an implementation will be deemed satisfactory. It can be surprising to see the acceptance criteria in a separate chapter. Agile method advocates would recommend attaching criteria directly to their corresponding requirements. It is also our recommendation. The traceability link between a requirement and its validation criteria should be made one way or the other. This section allows us to group them, as a dedicated group of people often take care of them.

```
Verification and acceptance criteria for an online
   Library Management System should ensure that the
   system meets its requirements and performs as
   expected.
Example of Verification criteria: The system responds
   to user actions within an acceptable time frame
   (search results within 2 s).
Example of Acceptance criteria: Users from each user
   role (librarian, patron) have tested the system
   and confirmed it meets their needs.
```

2.2.6 Project

The Project book describes all the constraints and expectations not about the system itself but about how to develop and produce it. It is composed of seven chapters.

P.1 Roles and Personnel

```
The main responsibilities in the LMS project are
   Project Manager, Testers, Documenters, and
   Developers.
They are described by Project requirements such as:
   - The project team includes a project manager and
     three systems engineers 100% dedicated to the
     project.
   - The team has to plan to test the product with the
     library manager as a super user able to switch
     from one role to another one to ensure the cor-
     rectness and safety of the developed software.
```

This chapter synthesizes the main responsibilities of the project, the required project staff, and their needed qualifications. The RACI chart is a concrete and classical tool often used to formalize those aspects, as illustrated in Fig. 2.22. A RACI chart, a responsibility assignment matrix, is a visual tool used in project management to delineate team roles clearly. It defines four distinct categories for each task, milestone, or decision:

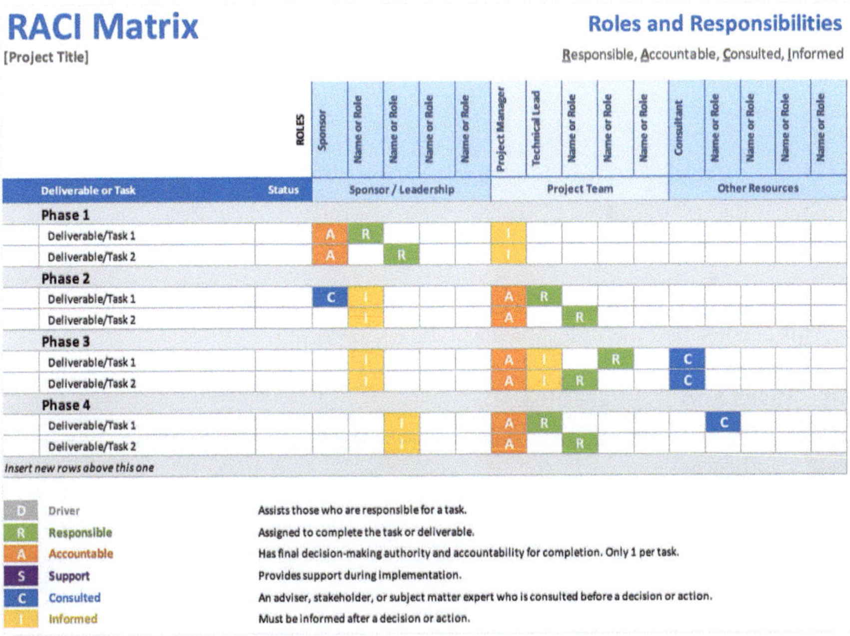

Fig. 2.22 An example of RACI chart

- **R**esponsible: The individual primarily accountable for completing the task
- **A**ccountable: The person who ultimately owns the decision or outcome
- **C**onsulted: Individuals whose input and expertise are valued and sought
- **I**nformed: Those who need to be updated on progress and decisions

By establishing these roles, RACI charts help prevent confusion, ensure accountability, and facilitate effective teamwork throughout a project.

Most of the requirements in this chapter will be of kind **role**.

P.2 Imposed Technical Choices

```
Users may access LMS from any device that has
Internet-browsing capabilities and an Internet
connection.
```

This chapter lists the imposed technical choices and any a priori choices that bind the project to specific tools, hardware, languages, or other technical parameters.

P.3 Schedule and Milestones

This chapter should not be empty (following the *Minimum Requirements Outcome Principle*).

```
One of the requirements of the project concerns its
   milestones:
The project should provide a first prototype (v.1) on
   May, 30, 2024.
```

This chapter lists the milestones and their scheduling.

P.4 Tasks and Deliverables

This chapter should not be empty (following the *Minimum Requirements Outcome Principle*).

```
The tasks and deliverables of the LMS are listed in
the Gantt diagram provided in Appendix XYZ.
```

2.2 Standard Plan for Requirements

This chapter gives details of individual **tasks** listed under **P.3—Schedule and Milestones** and their expected outcomes.

P.5 Required Technology Elements

```
The LMS realization imposes MongoDB for the database
and Maven for the project management.
```

This chapter details external systems, hardware, and software, expected to be necessary for building the system.

P.6 Risk and Mitigation Analysis

```
In an LMS, a potential obstacle to meeting the P.4
   schedule lies in the availability of a site
   provider.
The search for a hosting provider must be carried out
   at the very start of the project, and this phase
   must be added to the schedule.
```

This chapter details the potential obstacles to meeting the schedule of **P.4—Tasks and Deliverables** and measures for adapting the plan if they arise.

 Some critical projects could make this chapter mandatory.

P.7 Requirements Process and Report

```
The LMS project utilizes the PEGS approach to
   requirements.
Requirements are developed incrementally and allo-
   cated to one of the four books.
The process is conducted in an agile way.
```

In the initial version of the Project book, this chapter describes the requirements process. Later, it reports on its steps.

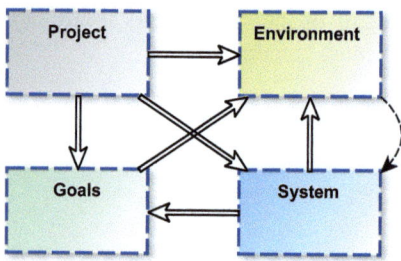

Fig. 2.23 Reference links

2.2.7 Links Between the Four PEGS

Figure 2.23 illustrates the dependability links between the four books. The dashed arrow[1] means "may reference."

One of the benefits of the organization in four books is that it supports a very precise separation of concerns. In particular, the requirements that are in the Goals book should not address any Project requirements as those are completely independent of the Goals. Similarly, System requirements should neither address any project requirements for the same reason. For example, the following requirement should raise a warning. Indeed, there should not be any reference to the Project book in a System requirement.

> S.1.23. The LMS has four components: Books Management, Patrons Management, Holds Management, and Checkouts Management (see P.4.16 for schedules).

In Sect. 4.1, we present an example of a concrete implementation of those dependability links in the form of an automated checking the undesired references are not present in the books (e.g., a Goals requirement referencing a System one).

In terms of verification obligations, the organization in books supports, here again, a clear separation of concerns. Figure 2.24 illustrates the verification obligations between the four books. The Environment requirements, being **assumptions** and **constraints**, have no obligations. However, the **system** should satisfy the requirements in the Goals and Environment books, while the Project requirements should satisfy (in that particular context, meaning "should serve") the **system**.

 The tools (theorem proving, model checking, simulations, etc.) used to verify the satisfaction of these obligations are out of this book's scope. Interested readers should refer to **The Handbook** chapter on formal requirements or to articles from the authors (ACM Survey 2021).

---

[1] Classical representation of dependency in software engineering (e.g., in UML)

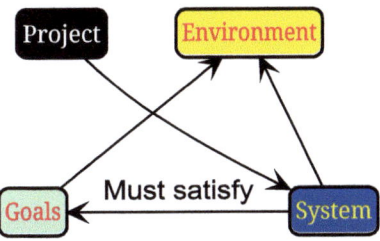

Fig. 2.24 Verification obligations

2.3 The Life Cycle Model

The Handbook is not prescriptive about the method to follow for requirements engineering. Nevertheless, it provides a typical life cycle associated with the concepts of OO requirements that we advise you to follow (see overview in Fig. 2.25 and Chap. 3).

The approach is divided into two main steps described below.

2.3.1 The Definition Step

The definition step corresponds to the production of the four PEGS. We advocate starting (in parallel) with the definition of the system's goals (task Define goals) and **environment** (task Analyse environment) through stakeholders' interviews and meetings. After these two initial tasks, the three main books (Goals, Environment, and System) should be in their initial version.

The next two tasks aim to plan the development and production of the Project book (task Plan project) and refine the System book by defining solution-oriented **components** (task Define clusters). A **cluster** is a coherent set of classes (components) whose development should be considered synchronously.

Even at this early stage, some verification (task Verify) can be performed as illustrated in Chap. 4.

2.3.2 The Implementation Step

Each identified cluster can now be developed in a classical way (represented as a mini V cycle, detailed in Fig. 2.26).

 The initial steps of this development are illustrated in Chap. 3.

The "Cluster model," detailed in chapter 12.5 of **The Handbook**, retains the sequential process of the Waterfall but without its synchronous nature. Each cluster (or subsystem) is developed from its related requirements in parallel with other clusters (e.g., as features in an Agile approach).

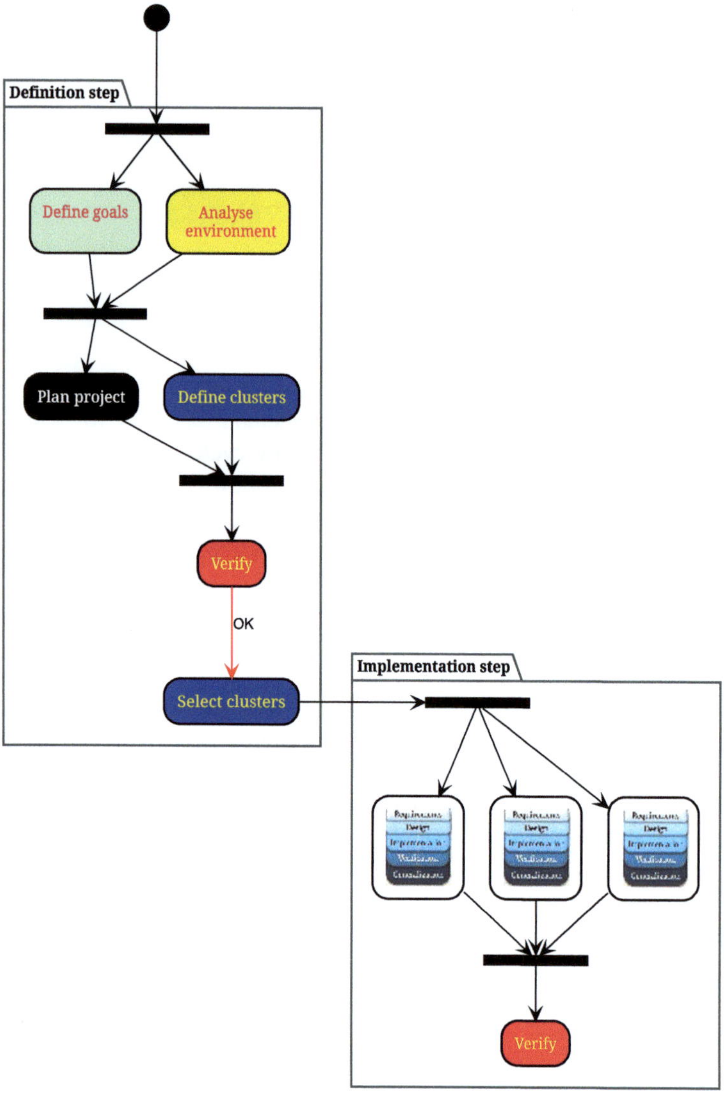

Fig. 2.25 The life cycle model

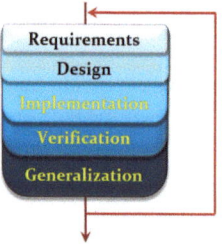

Fig. 2.26 Seamless development of a cluster

To decrease risks, the recommended order of starting clusters is from more fundamental and hardest to more secondary and easiest.

Finally, let us recall one of the principles that reflects the mix, adopted in PEGS, between the classical agile view of a single scheme for all sprints and the integration of the **RUP** and Waterfall ideas that are closer to real-life projects:

📕 **Not-All-Sprints-Are-Created-Equal ("NASACE")**
(see 12.7.2 of **The Handbook***)*

1. Every sprint includes a definition phase and an implementation phase.
2. Both of these phases involve verification.
3. Definition dominates early sprints and decreases afterward.
4. Implementation starts on a small scale with the earliest sprints and increases afterward.
5. Verification becomes dominant in the latest sprints.

2.4 Frontier Between Requirements and Analysis

2.4.1 Design Versus Requirements

Some parts of the standard plan could lead to overspecifications. For example, the **S.1—Component** chapter may contain preliminary definitions or lists of **components** resulting from design choices. The qualitative attribute of **abstractness** (and the associated **Requirements Abstraction Principle**) is defined to avoid such premature design or implementation decisions.

 In the classification of requirements elements, overspecification is a form of **noise**.

Many people are more comfortable thinking about how things work (operational thinking) than describing what things should do (descriptive specifications). Requirements engineers and business analysts should be trained to resist the urge to think operationally and instead produce unbiased specifications that accurately reflect the needs of the stakeholders.

 When relating a requirement with an existing one, you should always wonder if you *refine* (e.g., being more precise, making a vague requirement testable, etc.) or if you *implement* (making a preliminary design choice).

2.4.2 About Versioning and Variability

We have advocated for an iterative approach (see Sect. 2.3), starting with a first version (where non-conformance to the principles is allowed) and extending and revising it throughout the project. This implies maintaining the requirements the same way software is maintained nowadays: with a decent configuration management system that supports precise versioning for requirements and variability (e.g., for later decisions between variants of the product).

2.4.3 What About Requirement Attributes?

In many approaches and companies, well-formed requirements should have descriptive attributes (id, author, etc.). The PEGS is not prescriptive in that matter, but if the requirements have to be stored in a database or as objects, your organization must define its own set of important attributes to characterize them.

Here are some examples of classical requirements attributes (taken from (ISO-29148)):

Identification
Each requirement should be uniquely identified (i.e., number, name tag, mnemonic).

 See the **Identification Principle**.

Stakeholder Priority
The priority of each requirement should be identified (e.g., a scale such as 1–5 or a high/medium/low value or **MoSCoW**).

 While specific to some requirements, the **S.5—Prioritization** chapter can serve this purpose.

Dependency
The dependency between requirements, when it exists, should be made explicit.

Risk/Difficulty
Risk analysis techniques can be used to determine a grading for system requirements in terms of their consequences or degree of risk avoidance. The difficulty is an additional help in estimating costs.

 The **P.6—Risk and Mitigation Analysis** chapter can regroup those elements.

2.4 Frontier Between Requirements and Analysis

Source

Each requirement should include an attribute that indicates the originator.

Rationale

The rationale for establishing each requirement should be captured. In PEGS, we use the term **justification**.

Type

As we have shown in Sect. 2.1.3, requirements vary in intent and in the kinds of properties they represent.

Object-Oriented Requirements

Prerequisite

This chapter might be the most technical one and will require not only knowing the approach explained in Chap. 2 but also having a minimum of object-oriented (OO) programming knowledge. Object-oriented analysis and design are well-known concepts popularized by the works of B. Meyer, I. Jacobson, G. Booch, J. Rumbaugh, and others. Object-oriented (OO) programming is the dominant programming paradigm for enterprise applications. Object-oriented requirements structure the system description around types of objects manipulated by the system rather than operations performed by the system. This description is captured by classes, each corresponding to an object type.

What You Will Find in This Chapter

As described in **The Handbook**, the advantages of object-oriented technology also apply to requirements. In this chapter, we explore the application of OO techniques to requirements and use concrete examples taken from the Library Management System (LMS, detailed in Sect. 5.1). The lean transformation from requirements to code implementation is explained. It allows us to illustrate the round trip between implementation and requirements.

What You Will Not Find in This Chapter

Only the initial steps are explained. We do not provide in this **companion book** the full version of the code.

 Since classes capture the requirements, an object-oriented programming language can be used as a single notation from requirements to design and implementation. In this book, similarly to **The Handbook**, we use the Eiffel language for expressing requirements due to its readability and native support of contracts.

The approach to object-oriented requirements presented in this chapter goes beyond the material of chapter 8 of **The Handbook**.

3.1 Main Concepts

Since we are going to apply OO requirements to extended examples in the rest of this book, here is a recap of the key concepts. They include class, deferred versus effective, inheritance, and contracts.

3.1.1 Class as the Core Concept of OO Requirements

The core idea of object-oriented modeling (including OO requirements, OO design, OO programming, and other applications, collectively called "object technology") is to describe systems through the objects they manipulate and to express this description in terms of the operations applicable to objects and the properties of these operations (and not, e.g., in terms of the objects' physical representations). A class is a type of potential objects characterized by their operations (also called "features" or "methods") and associated properties (also called "contracts"). "Class" is the central concept of object technology, and an OO model is defined by a set of classes and their interconnections.

In the Library Management System (LMS for short, see Sect. 5.1 for more details), typical classes may include BOOK, PATRON, and CATALOG. The system manipulates objects (instances of these classes) during its operation. In the example, such objects will be computer representations of books kept in the library, library patrons, the library's catalog, and other library objects, physical or conceptual.

Object technology supports modeling systems at various levels of abstraction. In particular, a feature or a class may be either **effective** or **deferred**. "Effective" means fully implemented (and ready to execute as part of a program). A feature or class is "deferred" if its definition does not include an implementation or (for a class) includes a partial implementation only; it may still, however, include an abstract specification of the properties of the feature or class in the form of a "contract" as explained below. Deferred features and classes are particularly useful for requirements since requirements focus on specifying **behavior** rather than implementing it. For example, LIBRARY_ITEM may be a deferred class since it describes an abstract concept with several possible concrete realizations, such as BOOK and MAGAZINE (Fig. 3.1).

 We use **UML** class diagrams to illustrate the concepts.

3.1 Main Concepts

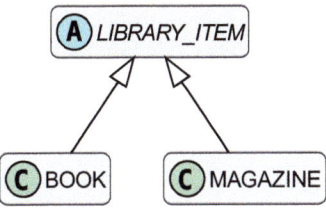

Fig. 3.1 The inheritance relationship between classes

Data types' properties are defined through operations: queries and commands. Queries provide information about objects, whereas commands update the corresponding objects.

3.1.2 Relations Between Classes

The OO model has two types of relations between classes: client and inheritance. A class C is a client of a class S if the features of C may use objects of type S. S is called a supplier of class C. In the LMS example, the class PATRON is a client of the class BOOK since the `place_hold` operation of PATRON relies on the instances of BOOK (see Fig. 3.2).

When a class H inherits from a class P, it has all the features and properties of P and can add its own features and properties. H is called an heir of P, and P is called a parent (a "superclass" in some programming languages) of H. In OO requirements, an heir H describes a specialized version of its parent P. In the LMS example, a library may have several item types, such as books and magazines, with different restrictions. In that case, classes BOOK and MAGAZINE will inherit from the class LIBRARY_ITEM, whereas class LIBRARY_ITEM will capture features and properties applicable to all item types (see Fig. 3.1).

In the case of multiple inheritance, the heir inherits from two or more different parents.

 Inheritance relations must always be acyclic, whereas Client relations can be cyclic.

3.1.3 Contracts

Specifying the properties of systems and their objects through the list of associated classes and their features only gives structural properties. To provide the actual

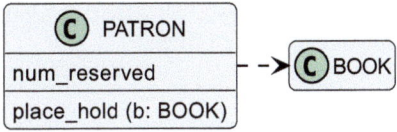

Fig. 3.2 The client relationship between classes

semantics of these elements—other than through the implementation—we should also express their abstract properties. Contracts fulfill this need. They include:

- The **precondition** of a feature, specifying the conditions under which it can be used
- Also for a feature, the **postcondition**, expressing properties resulting from its application
- For a class, the **class invariant**, expressing consistency properties applicable to all objects ("instances") of the class

Such a contract element consists of assertions, each of which is an individual Boolean **property** applicable to the corresponding objects, such as (for a BOOK instance, for example) "the book is currently on loan."

The example below demonstrates the roles of preconditions, postconditions, and class invariants:

```
class PATRON
feature
    num_reserved: INTEGER
    place_hold (b: BOOK)
        require
            num_reserved < 5
            b.is_available
        do
            -- Future implementation here
        ensure
            b.is_reserved (Current)
            num_reserved = old num_reserved + 1
        end
invariant
    valid_num_reserved_books: 0 <= num_reserved and num_reserved <= 5
end
```

The PATRON class code in Eiffel

- The `require` clause introduces a precondition of a feature `place_hold` of a class PATRON. It states that a patron must have at most 5 reserved books and can place a hold only on the available book when placing a hold.
- The `ensure` clause introduces a postcondition of a feature `place_hold`. It states that after placing a hold, a book's status must be `on_hold`, and the number of books reserved by a patron must increase by 1. The `invariant` clause introduces a class invariant that states that a patron's number of books reserved must be between 0 and 5 at any given time.

3.1 Main Concepts

A **Specification driver** is a contracted routine, expressed only in terms of its formal arguments, that serves specification purposes. Specification drivers take objects to be specified as arguments and express the effect of operations on those objects with preconditions and postconditions. OO requirements rely on specification drivers for expressing scenarios (such as use cases) and tests.

Specification drivers can express properties that apply to several objects, possibly of different types. For example, "available books can be placed on hold by only one patron at any given time." To express the corresponding OO requirement, we may use the specification-driver assertion, which describes a generic scenario of using the relevant features and specifies its effect through the postcondition, as presented in the listing below:

```
holding_available_book_by_two_patrons (b: BOOK; p1, p2: PATRON; l:
LIBRARY)
    require
        b.is_available
        p1 /= p2
        l.has_patron (p1)
        l.has_patron (p2)
    do
        l.place_book_on_hold (b, p1)
        l.place_book_on_hold (b, p2)
    ensure
        l.book_is_on_hold (b, p1)
        not l.book_is_on_hold (b, p2)
    end
```

In this example, the precondition states that:

- Before placing a hold, a book must be available.
- We consider two different patrons.
- Both patrons should be registered in a library.

The postcondition states that after two patrons attempt to place a hold on a book, the first patron will place the book on hold, not the second one. As the values b, p1, and p2 are passed as parameters, the correct implementation of the feature place_book_on_hold will imply that calling the feature holding_available_book_by_two_patrons with parameters that satisfy the preconditions will not cause a contract violation.

Specification drivers retain the OO style of requirements specification but make it more general by covering arbitrary properties, not just those expressible within a single class of the original object-oriented model.

3.2 Producing OO Requirements

Object-oriented requirements modeling relies on the following concepts:

- Object types, described through applicable operations—queries (providing information) and commands (updating information)
- Software contracts, which capture the semantics of operations

There are three dimensions of object-oriented requirements specification: an object model, a functional specification, and a behavioral specification.

The **object model** captures key abstractions in the application domain in the form of classes. This static model aims to specify abstract data types for all relevant environmental phenomena.

The **functional specification** provides a specification of individual operations. Operations correspond to features of classes of the object model. Their abstract specification relies on in-class contracts.

Behavioral specification defines permissible sequences of operations. Behavioral specification relies on the following mechanisms:

- **Specification drivers** capture scenarios as example sequences of operations and may serve testing purposes.
- **Software contracts** provide abstract specification of time-ordering constraints.

3.2.1 How to Produce Object-Oriented Requirements

Once adopted, the object-oriented approach pervades the whole process of requirements elicitation and analysis. In other words, the idea is not to produce some traditional kind of requirements and then make the result object-oriented; instead, OO principles help structure the entire effort by providing a unifying conceptual framework for describing the system and its environment.

Although the process is iterative, we can list its basic steps:

1. Eliciting and documenting requirements.
2. Drafting OO model: OO model captures the key components of the system and its environment with classes, linked with client and inheritance relations.
3. Producing functional OO requirements: Functional OO specification enriches the OO model with features, expressing functional requirements, and their contracts, expressing environment properties and constraints.
4. Producing OO behavioral specification: Abstract properties of system's functions (such as time-ordering constraints) are extracted from scenarios.

3.2.2 Eliciting and Documenting Requirements

The key books containing information for OO requirements are the Environment and System books. Chapter **E.2**, **Components** of the Environment book, lists the **environment** components. Each **component** corresponds to a class. Similarly, software components, listed in chapter **S.1**, **Components** of the System book, correspond to their respective classes. All these classes, clients, inheritance relationships, and software contracts form an object-oriented requirements model. This model is further enriched with scenario classes, which model use cases or use case stories as **specification drivers**.

3.2.3 Modeling Components of the System and Its Environment

A requirements engineer should describe key abstractions in the application domain through classes to produce an object model. These classes should cover both the system and its environment. In the LMS case study, examples of such classes are LIBRARY (system class), BOOK, and PATRON (environment classes).

 You can use colors or stereotypes in **UML** to represent the categories of a class (Fig. 3.3).

We can take advantage of inheritance to organize the description of these concepts into hierarchies, for example:

- Library items can be of different types, such as books and magazines. In that case, a deferred class LIBRARY_ITEM will describe an abstract concept of a library item, whereas classes BOOK and MAGAZINE will provide its concrete implementations.

Fig. 3.3 Stereotypes or colors express Categories of classes

- There could be two categories of patrons: regular and research patrons with different restrictions, such as the number of books on hold or a hold duration. In that case, classes `REGULAR_PATRON` and `RESEARCH_PATRON` would inherit from the class `PATRON`, which captures features applicable to all patrons.

Further development of OO requirements will enrich the classes of OO model with features corresponding to applicable operations and contracts, providing abstract specifications of operations.

3.2.4 Producing Functional Specification

In object-oriented requirements, elements of system functionality (system features) correspond to features (procedures) of classes. The properties of those operations are captured with software contracts. Consider the following requirement:

```
S.2.1.3 The Library Management System shall provide
the ability to place a hold on books.
```

To express this requirement in an object-oriented style, we add the feature `reserve_a_book (p: PATRON; b: BOOK)` to the `LIBRARY` class:

```
reserve_a_book (p: PATRON; b: BOOK)
    deferred
    end
```

Further refinement of this feature comes from the constraints:

```
S.2.1.3.1 If placing hold is not allowed, the
   reserve_a_book operation shall keep the number of
   reserved books unchanged for a given patron.
S.2.1.3.2 If placing hold is allowed, the reserve_a_
   book operation shall increase the number of reserved
   books by 1 for a given patron.
```

Initially, we can add it to object-oriented requirements simply as a contract's tag:

3.2 Producing OO Requirements

```
class LIBRARY feature
    reserve_a_book (p: PATRON; b: BOOK)
        deferred
        ensure
            S_2_1_3_1_unsuccessful_hold:
            S_2_1_3_2_successful_hold:
        end
end
```

Such an implementation is valid and will not cause compilation errors. Nevertheless, to fully exploit the benefits of object-oriented requirements, the next refinement step would express the constraints S.2.1.3.1 and S.2.1.3.2 in a programming language:

```
class LIBRARY feature
    reserve_a_book (p: PATRON; b: BOOK)
    deferred
    ensure
        S_2_1_3_1_unsuccessful_hold: not hold_is_allowed(p,b) implies
            p.num_reserved = old p.num_reserved
        S_2_1_3_2_successful_hold: hold_is_allowed(p,b) implies
            p.num_reserved = old p.num_reserved + 1
    end
end
```

We further link the natural language requirement, stored in text format, with an object-oriented requirement, expressed in a programming language, by adding a hyperlink to a requirements document and an annotation to the respective requirements class (see Fig. 3.4). Clicking the hyperlink from the class code will open the requirements document at the bookmark, which corresponds to the respective requirement. Clicking the hyperlink in the requirements document will open the source code of the feature specified by the given requirement.

3.2.5 Behavioral Specification

A scenario is a pattern of exercising the features (operations) of one or more classes; the use cases have little to do with object orientation since they are essentially procedural. Nevertheless, they play a complementary role and serve elicitation and testing purposes. According to the use case 2.0 approach (a successor of the use-case-driven approach developed by Ivar Jacobson), use case stories play a key role

```
class
    LIBRARY

feature
    reserve_a_book (p: PATRON; b: BOOK)
        -- Reserve a book b by patron p
        note
            EIS: "protocol=DOC", "src=C:\Documents\LMS Requirements document.docx",
                 "name=If a patron has less than five holds, placing a hold is successful
                 "bookmark=If_a_patron_has_less_than_five_holds_p1"
            EIS: "protocol=DOC", "src=C:\Documents\LMS Requirements document.docx",
                 "name=If a patron has five holds, placing a hold is not successful, and
                 "bookmark=If_a_patron_has_five_holds_placing_a_hol"
        require
            has_patron (p)
            has_book (b)
        do
        ensure
            S_2_1_3_1_unsuccessful_hold: not hold_is_allowed(p,b) implies
                                         p.num_reserved = old p.num_reserved
            S_2_1_3_2_successful_hold: hold_is_allowed(p,b) implies
                                       p.num_reserved = old p.num_reserved + 1
        end
```

Fig. 3.4 Hyperlinks in action

in behavioral specification. A story describes a possible path through a use case that is of value to a user or other stakeholder.

In OO requirements, a story is simply a routine exercising the features of the respective classes. The routines, specifying a set of related use case stories, can be grouped in a separate class. In that case, a story is a typical instance of the concept of specification driver.

Here is a general use case stories class exercising features of classes BOOK, PATRON, and LIBRARY:

```
class LIBRARY_BOOK_USAGE_STORIES feature

    reserve_book_successfully (b: BOOK; lb: LIBRARY; p: PATRON)
        require
            p.num_reserved < 5
            b.is_available
        do
            lb.reserve_a_book (b, p)
        ensure
        b.is_reserved (p)
        end

    holding_available_book_by_two_patrons(b: BOOK; p1, p2: PATRON; l: LIBRARY)
            -- As presented above

    reserve_book_num_holds_exceeded (b: BOOK; lb: LIBRARY; p: PATRON)
            -- Specification of the use case story

    -- Other use case stories
end
```

Use case stories, expressed in OO style, also serve as test cases. When actual arguments are passed, use case stories become tests.

3.3 Requirements Traceability

Since OO requirements are code artifacts, they can be directly linked to the other code elements and external documents. OO requirements traceability is maintained with the following mechanisms:

- Inheritance relationships link requirements classes to implementation classes. The software development process consists of refinement steps. The initial requirements model consists of deferred classes that describe important abstractions of the problem domain but do not provide implementation details. Implementation classes inherit from requirements classes and provide an implementation that satisfies contracts.
- Client relationships link requirements classes with the corresponding scenario classes.
- The Integrated Development Environment (IDE) provides facilities to create and maintain links with artifacts outside of the IDE:
  - Functional requirements, such as "The Library Management System shall provide the ability to place a hold on books," can be linked to the respective features of classes, specifying respective modules.
  - The abstract specification of system features, such as "A regular patron is limited to five holds at any given moment," is expressed with contracts that can be traced to the corresponding procedures.

A more detailed illustration of the traceability links is provided in the complete Roborace specification (see Sect. 5.3).

Quality and Verification Criteria for Requirements

4

Prerequisite

This chapter provides some implementation examples of the verification rules that can be found in **The Handbook**. Some of them can only be manually checked, but most of them can be implemented according to a specific environment.

What You Will Find in This Chapter

The following sections illustrate such possible implementations. They have to be taken more as examples than prescriptions but are illustrative of the benefits of having a strict and well-organized requirements engineering approach.

What You Will Not Find in This Chapter

We have not implemented all the principles. The comprehensive list of all the principles we have extracted from **The Handbook** can be found in **Appendix D**.

4.1 Books Mutual References

One of the requirements for this book, taken from **The Handbook**, says (see **here**):

> The books may reference each other, but not arbitrarily.

Figure 4.1 shows which books may refer to which.
Here are some explanations:

1. The Project book may refer to all the others, as the outcomes from the three others can be considered as artifacts produced by some steps, which might be described in the Project book.

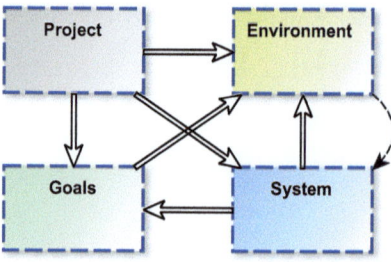

Fig. 4.1 Possible references between the books

```
#-------------------------------------------------
# language: en
Feature: Book mutual references
    The books should follow the mutual references rules.

Scenario: The Environment book must not refer to the Goals and Project books
    Given The Environment book
    Then No reference should include the Goals book
    And No reference should include the Project book
    And Only E.5 section can refer to the System book

Scenario: The Goals book must not refer to the Project and System books
    Given The Goals book
    Then No reference should include the Project book
    And No reference should include the System book

Scenario: The System book must not refer to the Project book
    Given The System book
    Then No reference should include the Project book
```

Fig. 4.2 Verification rule as a BDD feature

2. The Goals book must be self-contained. This is somehow an adaptation of the "Separation of Concerns," where the idea is to separate the problem space from the solution space. There might be some references to the Environment though, as some parts of the objectives might have some dependencies.
3. The System book will often refer to the Environment book (especially assumptions and constraints) as well as to the Goals book (for traceability and justification purposes). But it must not refer to the Project book, since it is necessary to describe the system independently of when and how it will be developed.
4. The dotted arrow signals that the Environment book may refer to the System to describe possible changes to the environment's properties caused by the system. Such cases may appear only in Chapters E.5 and E.6 ("Effects" and "Invariants") of the Environment book.

From this mutual references rule, a concrete implementation, written in Gherkin, enforces its application (Figs. 4.2 and 4.3):

Here is the execution, using cucumber, of the corresponding tests, showing that they all pass (green lines):

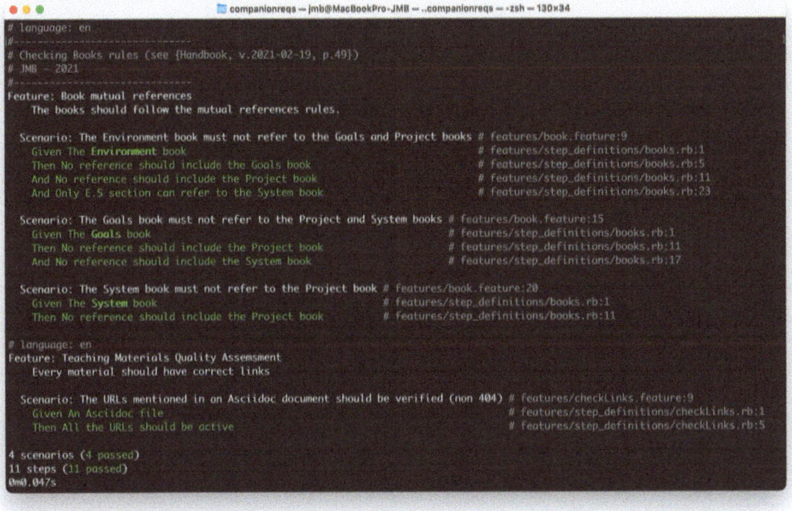

Fig. 4.3 Tests execution

4.2 The "To Be Determined" Rule

Writing requirements can lead to questions and uncertainty, requiring more information (mostly from some stakeholders) to be completed. TBD (*To Be Determined*) can then appear here and there in the preliminary versions of the requirements. The TBD rule (see **The Handbook**, p. 92) explains that any incomplete mention in requirements must include:
1. Name of author declaring the property "TBD"
2. Date the property was found to be "TBD"
3. Date or project phase by which the indetermination should be resolved
4. Importance of resolving it, one of showstopper, serious, or desirable
5. What will be needed to resolve it, one or more of stakeholders to ask, documentation to consider, or management decision (by whom)

In addition, the requirements must include a TBD list with links to all TBDs.

Example 1 TBD Details

> Triggering conditions for overheating alarm: TBD.
> 1. Introduced by: Bertrand Meyer
> 2. On: 2021-09-10
> 3. Importance: serious
> 4. Resolve before: the start of any coding of the alarm management module.
> 5. To resolve:
>   - Stakeholders: heating control engineers
>   - Documents: heating system manual (version 4, expected 2021-10-10).

We have implemented an illustration of such rule enforcement in the form of an issue template. In the context of a GitHub development, issues can be considered as requirements.[1] In this implementation, the rule is the following: before writing any "TBD" in an issue, you should first write the details of this TBD (see Fig. 4.4) and then refer to it (see Fig. 4.5).

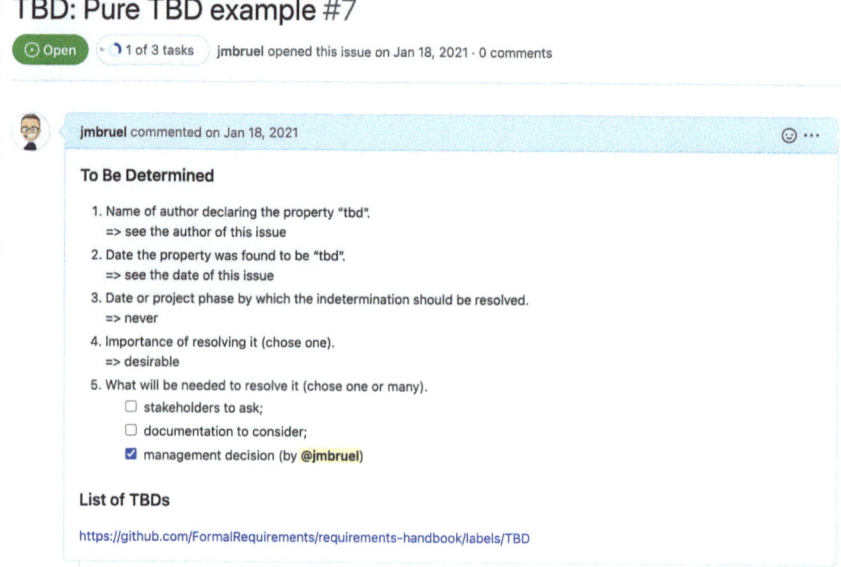

Fig. 4.4 Example of a To Be Determined details definition as an issue (#7)

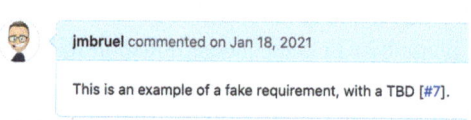

Fig. 4.5 Example of a To Be Determined reference

---

[1] We also provide an implementation of the PEGS if you want to express requirements using issues; see **Appendix E**.

4.4 GitHub Implementation Example

```
1  #-------------------------------
2  # Checking The Minimum Requirements Outcome Principle (see {Handbook, p.27})
3  # JMB - 2023
4  #-------------------------------
5  # language: en
6  Feature: Minimum Requirements Outcome Principle
7      The requirements effort must always produce the following elements.
8
9  Scenario: The Project book must have P3 P4 chapters
10     Given The Project book
11     Then P3 chapter must not be empty
12     And P4 chapter must not be empty
13
14 Scenario: The Environment book must have E3 chapter
15     Given The Environment book
16     Then E3 chapter must not be empty
17
18 Scenario: The Goals book must have G1 G3 G7 chapters
19     Given The Goals book
20     Then G1 chapter must not be empty
21     And G3 chapter must not be empty
22     And G7 chapter must not be empty
23
24 Scenario: The System book must have S1 S2 chapters
25     Given The System book
26     Then S1 chapter must not be empty
27     And S2 chapter must not be empty
```

Fig. 4.6 The Minimum Requirements Outcome Principle as a BDD feature (see **source**)

4.3 The Minimum Requirements Outcome Principle

This principle (see **Minimum Requirements Outcomes Principle**) lists the minimal content of any decent requirements documentation. This is pretty easy to implement. In our **Cucumber** implementation, we simply verify that those sections are not empty (Fig. 4.6).

4.4 GitHub Implementation Example

This part illustrates the use of PEGS in the context of ◯ **GitHub**. Following the **Requirements Nature Principle**, requirements, as any other software artifact, can be stored and managed in a ◯ **GitHub** repository as `issues`.

The GitHub template we are providing in the **companion website** (available directly at https://github.com/FormalRequirements/HandBookTemplate/) contains not only the standard plan but also examples of ways to express requirements as issues directly.

Kinds of Requirements

As illustrated in Fig. 1.3, it is easy to define specific labels to tag the requirements according, for example, to the book they are part of. We have defined an initial set of labels (that even respect the standard four PEGS colors) that can easily be extended (see Fig. 4.7).

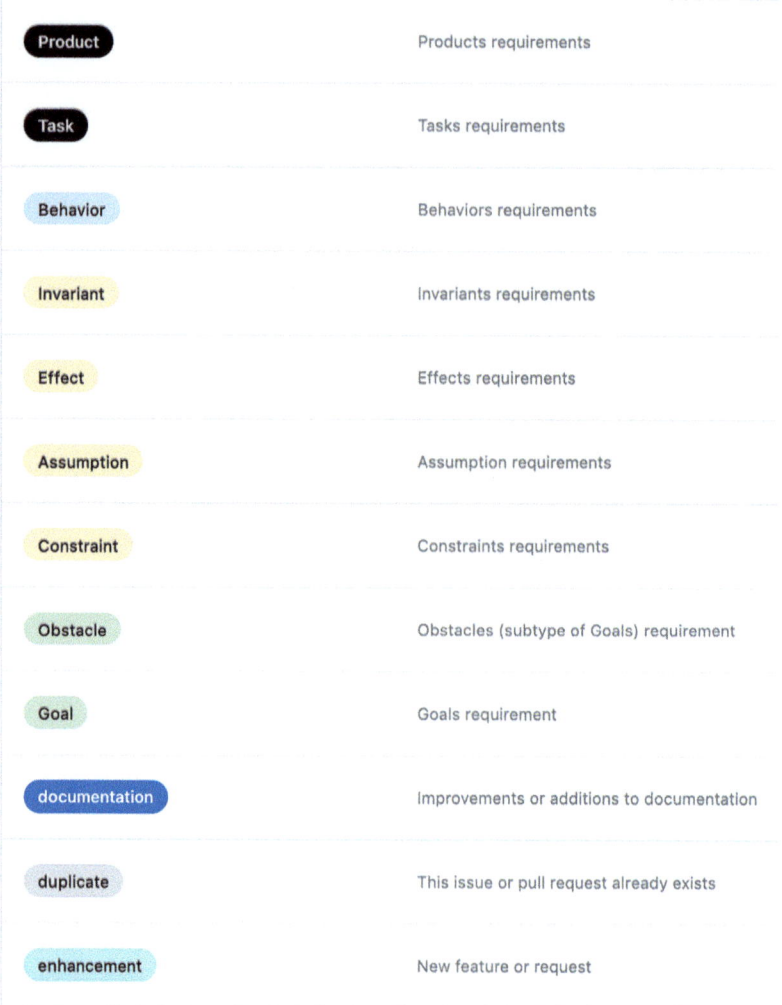

Fig. 4.7 Labels to tag requirements by kind

Templates for Requirements

Thanks to GitHub's issue templating, a unified form for specific requirements can be provided. Figures 4.8, 4.9, and 4.10 illustrate our template for "To be determined" requirements.

4.4 GitHub Implementation Example

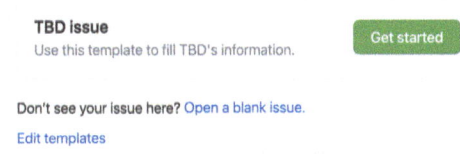

Fig. 4.8 TBD template

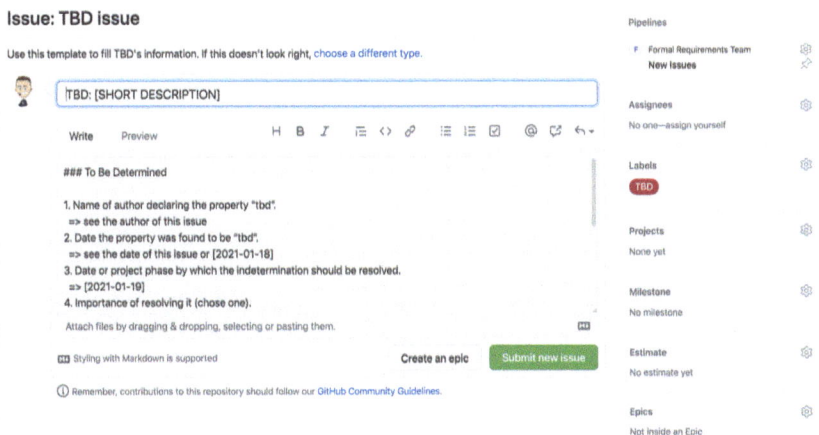

Fig. 4.9 TBD being filled

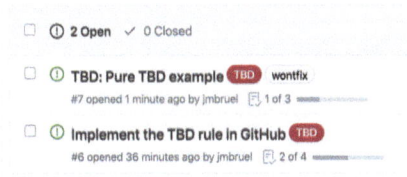

Fig. 4.10 TBDs list

Organization in Chapters

Thanks to the notion of `Project`, where issues can be sorted, listed, and organized, our GitHub template provides a ready-to-use project organized in chapters following the standard plan (see Fig. 4.11).

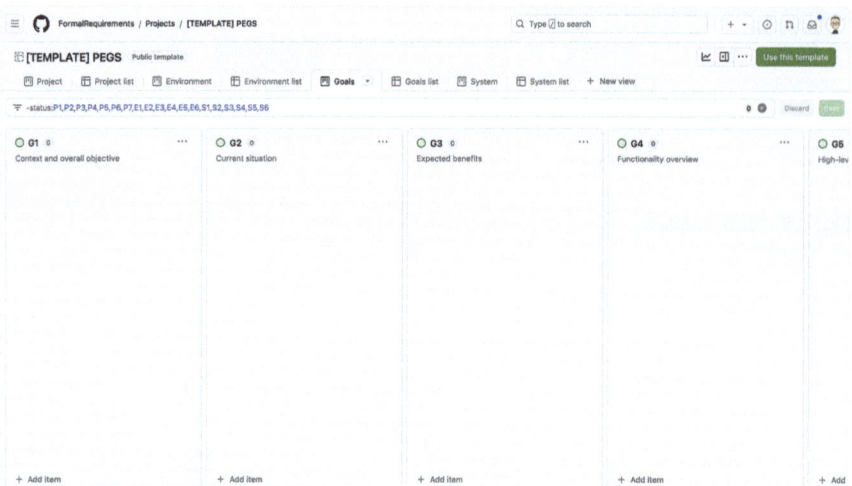

Fig. 4.11 Project as a way to organize requirements in chapters

Table 4.1 High-level guidelines toward requirements engineering

Ref.	Description	Handbook
[REQ-M1]	Define a standard document structure	✔ (see Sect. 2.2)
[REQ-M2]	Make the document easy to change	✔ (see **Appendix E**)
[REQ-M3]	Uniquely identify each requirement	✔ (see **Identification principle**)
[REQ-M4]	Define policies for requirements management	
[REQ-M5]	Define standard templates for requirements description	✔ (see **Appendix E**)
[REQ-M6]	Use language simply, constantly, and concisely	
[REQ-M7]	Organize formal requirements inspections	✔ (see Sect. 2.3)
[REQ-M8]	Define validation checklists	
[REQ-M9]	Use checklists for requirements analysis	
[REQ-M10]	Plan for conflicts and conflict resolution	✔ (see Sect. 2.3)

4.5 Additional Guidelines for Quality

Appendix D lists all the 36 principles of **The Handbook**, whether they are covered by an above rule implementation (e.g., the **Minimum Requirements Outcomes Principle**) or not.

We would like to take the opportunity of this section to also mention a comprehensive list of useful guidelines, taken from Sommerville and Sawyer (2004) (we have ticked the one we believe PEGS supports) (Table 4.1).

Case Studies 5

▼ ⊘ *Corresponding Requirement*
This section satisfies requirements **G1.1** and **S.1.1.2** (see Sect. 5.2).

Prerequisite
This chapter provides concrete results of the PEGS approach. It is then recommended to read Chap. 2. The domains of those case studies do not require much background.

What You Will Find in This Chapter
We are detailing three case studies in this chapter:

- An information system of an imaginary Library context (called Library Management System)
- The production of a book (this **companion book**)
- A real-case race of self-driving cars (called Roborace)

 Each of the three authors of this **companion book** has performed a case study. They have been made individually and separately. Even if we have made reviews and discussions, we have intentionally left some differences in the style (e.g., the way requirements were numbered) or the level of detail.

What You Will Not Find in This Chapter
We had no room to detail the iterative versions of the four books. Nevertheless, those interested should contact the authors to access the repositories we used to realize them (containing the git history).

© The Author(s), under exclusive license to Springer Nature
Switzerland AG 2025
J.-M. Bruel et al., *Applying Requirements and Business Analysis*,
https://doi.org/10.1007/978-3-031-92160-5_5

5.1 A Library Management System (LMS)

Version: 2024-07-25
Changelog

2023-08-23	First proposition—by Sophie Ebersold
2023-08-24	Change version number, correct some typos, add some requirements in P.3 and P.4 to be consistent with the *Minimum Requirements Outcomes Principle*, put it in a Google doc form to ease collaboration—by J.-M. Bruel
2023-10-04	Change numbering, correct some typos—add explanations and reduce the number of requirements specified here, as they constitute examples of what has to be contained in each chapter, replace occurrences of members by patrons to avoid ambiguities—by Sophie Ebersold
2023-10-11	Add numbering, correct some typos—add explanations and reduce the number of requirements specified here, as they constitute examples of what has to be contained in each book, add in each chapter an explanation of how the chapter was completed—by Sophie Ebersold
2023-10-19	Correct numbering—move some requirements from E section to S section, move some requirements from E.4 Assumptions to E.3 Constraints, add new assumption in E.4, better specified some requirements—by Sophie Ebersold
2023-10-24	Add an assumption about **librarians accounts**—by Sophie Ebersold
2024-01-08	Add a note and a requirement in **E.3**—by Sophie Ebersold
2024-07-25	Typos, some re-numbering, ordering the Glossary E.1, change ToC—by J.-M. Bruel

5.1.1 Context

As an attempt to illustrate the general purpose of PEGS and to validate it on business systems, we have written the requirements of an online library management system. In the following, we will consider the Library Management System as being the system under specification and the system to develop. The Library Management System will also be called **LMS** in the rest of this document.

This document constitutes the full version of the requirements documentations of this system. It follows the method presented in **The Handbook**, specifying the requirements among four books: Goals, Environment, System, and Project.

It uses the AsciiDoc template available **here**.

In the following, we illustrate and discuss some of our choices, our hesitation, and the benefit of using PEGS in that software product.

 This shows the advantage of having a well-organized set of requirements for developing any new project. The requirements specified in the four PEGS books below were used by two groups of third year bachelor students to develop the corresponding online **LMS** tool.

5.1.2 Goals

The *Online* Library Management System is a solution to the challenges faced by libraries. It is designed to meet the primary goals of a Library Management System and can significantly benefit any library.

A **Library** has a collection of **Books** that its members can borrow.

Any existing or new **Library** can use the Library Management System to manage its **Books** (insertion, borrowing, and monitoring).

The Library Management System can work as a powerful library management system for big libraries and can provide a free, easy-to-use system for rising libraries.

 The Library Management System will also be called **LMS** in the following.

G.1 Context and Overall Objectives

 This chapter explains why the project is needed, recalls the business context, and presents the general business objectives.

G.1.1 The **LMS** is to be used by **Librarians** and **Patrons** of a **Library**.
G.1.2 The **LMS** should be accessible through the Internet.
G.1.3 All the functionalities of the **LMS** will be accessible through a graphical user interface.
G.1.4 The purpose of the **LMS** is to provide its users with a friendly environment.
G.1.5 The **LMS** manages **Book** borrowing.
G.1.6 The system provides **Books Catalog** and information to **Patrons** and helps them decide on the **Books** to borrow from the library.
G.1.7 The system provides reports to **Librarians** and helps them manage late loans.
G.1.8 The **LMS** runs 24 h a day.
G.1.9 Access to the **LMS** must be secured.

G.2 Current Situation

 This chapter describes the current situation and gives the relations between the **LMS** and its environment.

G.2.1 The **LMS** is described in this project, starting from scratch, based on a manual library management and various public resources such as **this one**.[1]

---

[1] https://github.com/ddd-by-examples/library?ref=hackernoon.com#domain-description

G.3 Expected Benefits

 New processes, or improvements to existing processes, made possible by the project's results (see **The Handbook**).

G.3.1 The **LMS** product is basically updating a manual library system into an Internet-based application.

G.3.2 The system should enable its users to access basic library functions remotely, 24 h a day, according to their role in the system.

G.3.3 The system should provide a **Catalog** and reports allowing users to improve their use of the **Library**.

G.3.4 Anyone should be able to register by creating his or her own account.

G.3.5 A user-friendly interface, online help, and user guide must be sufficient to educate the users on how to use this product without any problems or difficulties.

G.4 Functionality Overview

 This chapter gives a short overview of the future system. It lists the main functionalities a **LMS** must provide its users. It also says what users cannot do.

G.4.1 **Librarians** need to be able to add **Books**, update **Books** status, delete **Books**, and receive alerts on overdue returns.

G.4.2 **Librarians** are responsible for registering **Books Checkouts** and Returns.

G.4.3 **Patrons** should be able to remotely consult the library **Catalog**, put **Books** on hold, know the remaining time for borrowing, and update their personal information.

G.4.4 **Patrons** cannot update their borrowing information.

G.4.5 Only registered users should be able to access the system.

G.5 High-Level Usage Scenarios

 The scenarios chosen for appearing here are limited to the main usage patterns and expressed in user terms, independently of the system's structure. The detailed usage scenarios will appear in the System book (**S.4**). We consider here the two kinds of users the **LMS** has to integrate: **Librarians** and **Patrons**.

G.5.1 All users must authenticate themselves before using the system.

G.5.2 Each user must have his or her correct username and password to enter into his or her online account and do actions.

G.5.3 Librarians:

- G.5.3.1 Should be able to insert, modify the state of a Book, and delete Books
- G.5.3.2 Can get the information of any member who has borrowed a Book
- G.5.3.3 Add and edit **Book** categories and arrange **Books** by categories.
- G.5.3.4 Add and edit authors and publishers' information
- G.5.3.5 Can send warning to people who have exceeded deadline date
- G.5.3.6 Should enter **Book** checkouts and returns

G.5.4 Patrons:

- G.5.4.1 Should be able to subscribe.
- G.5.4.2 Should be provided with the updated information about the Books Catalog.
- G.5.4.3 Can check their account's information and update it.
- G.5.4.4 Have the ability to search through **Books** by subject, title, authors, or any information related to the **Book**.
- G.5.4.5 Can put **Books** on hold.

G.6 Limitations and Exclusions

Aspects that the system need not address (see **The Handbook**).

G.6.1 Accessibility issues are not considered by the **LMS**.
G.6.2 The **LMS** only deals with **Book** management and does not cover human resources management.
G.6.3 The **LMS** does not support users' validation.
G.6.4 The administration of the Web site is out of the scope of the system.

Patrons can create accounts, but **Librarians** cannot. The Web master is the only one able to create **Librarians** accounts (out of the scope of the system).

G.7 Stakeholders and Requirements Sources

Groups of people who can affect the project or be affected by it and other places to consider for information about the project and system (see **The Handbook**).

G.7.1 Stakeholders

Stakeholder	Category	Comment
Patron	User	Anyone who borrows **Books** in the **Library**
Librarian	User	Persons responsible for managing **Books** and loans

G.7.2 Resources

- https://github.com/ddd-by-examples/library#domain-description
- https://www.codingninjas.com/studio/library/design-a-library-management-system-low-level-design

5.1.3 Environment

 The Environment book describes the application domain and external context in which the **LMS** will operate.

E.1 Glossary

 Clear and precise definitions of all the vocabulary specific to the **LMS**, including technical terms, words from ordinary language used in a special meaning, and acronyms (see **The Handbook**).

E.1.1 The definitions of all the **LMS**-specific terms are given below.

 We have chosen to number all glossary entries, so that each can be referenced by its number, just like any other requirement in this **LMS** specification.

E.1.2 Book

Copy of a **Book** with a copy number and an availability status

E.1.3 Borrowing

Taking a **Book** from the **Library**

E.1.4 Borrowing Period

Period during which a **Book** can be borrowed

E.1.5 Catalog

List of **Library Books** and their instance availability

E.1.6 Checkout

Collecting a **Book** from the **Library**

E.1.7 Daily Sheet with Expired Holds

A list of expired holds that is being checked daily

E.1.8 Daily Sheet with Overdue Checkouts

A list of overdue **Checkouts** that is being checked daily

E.1.9 Holding

To place a **Book** on hold

E.1.10 Hold Duration

A time period when a **Book** can be kept on hold

E.1.11 ISBN

International Standard Book Number—uniquely identifies a monograph regardless of the publication medium.

E.1.12 Librarian

A **Library** employee.

E.1.13 Library

Has a collection of **Books** and members called **Patrons** and Librarians.

E.1.14 LMS

Acronym for Library Management System, the system under study in this case study

E.1.15 Meta Book

Metadata containing title, author, editor, **ISBN**, and number of copies

E.1.16 Overdue Checkout

A checkout is overdue when a **Patron** has not given the **Book** back until up to the **Borrowing Period**.

E.1.17 Patron

Anyone who borrows **Books** in the **Library**.

E.1.18 Return

Giving the **Book** back to the **Library**.

During the development of the system, we noticed that some members of the team did not know what an **ISBN** was and thought that there was one **ISBN** per physical **Book**. So we decided to add the definition of **ISBN** to the glossary.

E.2 Components

We list the elements of the environment that may affect or be affected by the system and project, that is, the login management component to which the system must be interfaced.

E.2.1 Login Management

E.2.1.1 This component would handle the login of the users (**Patrons** and **Librarians**) and their authentication.

E.2.1.2 It is not dedicated to a **Library** and can be an external module added to the **LMS**.

E.3 Constraints

This chapter will contain the obligations and limits imposed on the project and the system by the environment. It describes all the important business rules that the development of the **LMS** must consider. Some of them are given below.

E.3.1 A **Book** placed on hold and whose hold is not expired is unavailable.
E.3.2 A **Book** that has been checked out is unavailable.
E.3.3 A **Book** becomes available when the **Hold Duration** expires.
E.3.4 After a **Book** return is registered, the **Book** becomes available.
E.3.5 When a **Book** is checked out, the hold completes, and the returning process starts.
E.3.6 A **Patron** can place a hold on a **Book** if the **Book** is available.
E.3.7 A **Patron** is limited to ten holds at any moment.
E.3.8 **Overdue Checkouts** and expired holds are checked daily.
E.3.9 **Overdue Checkouts** are registered.
E.3.10 **Overdue Checkout** results in fees for the concerned, a penalty on his/her file, and emails.
E.3.11 If a checkout is overdue, it is being unregistered as soon as the **Book** is returned.
E.3.12 When an overdue **Book** is returned, collecting the penalty fee begins.
E.3.13 **Patrons** who are overdue with a current loan cannot borrow, even if their loan quota has not been reached.
E.3.14 **Patrons** who have not paid their penalty fee cannot borrow **Books**.
E.3.15 A **Patron** who has obtained the maximum number of penalties will be blacklisted by the library and banned from the system for 1 year.

Hold Duration was expressed in days, but we choose to express it in hours as "day" can be ambiguous and subject to interpretation.

E.3.16 **Hold Duration** is a maximum of 120 h.
E.3.17 **Borrowing Period** is a maximum of 60 days.
E.3.18 The maximum number of **Books** placed on hold by a single user is three.
E.3.19 The maximum number of **Books** borrowed by a single user is five.
E.3.20 Late-**Borrowing** fees are €5 per day.
E.3.21 The maximum number of penalties is three.
E.3.22 The maximum period for returning an overdue **Book** is 6 months. After this period, the user is deregistered, and an administrative procedure is launched.

5.1 A Library Management System (LMS)   75

During the development of the system, the team highlighted the problem of the frequency of notifications in the case of overdue: How often is a user notified that they are overdue? So, we added the following requirement.

E.3.23 When a **Patron** is overdue, a weekly notification is sent out by email (on Mondays), indicating the updated amount of the fees.

E.4 Assumptions

Below are some properties of the environment that may be assumed to facilitate the project and simplify the **LMS**.

E.4.1 The users can read French.
E.4.2 The users are assumed to have basic knowledge of computers and Internet browsing.
E.4.3 **Librarian** accounts are supposed to be created outside the application.

E.5 Effects

We have not found any elements and properties of the environment that the system will affect.

E.6 Invariants

Invariants describe properties of the environment that the **LMS**'s operation must preserve.

E.6.1 The following are the status a **Book** can have: `available`, `on hold`, `borrowed`, `due`, and `returned`.

5.1.4 System

The System book refines the Goals by focusing on more detailed requirements about the system under development, mainly its constituents, behaviors, and properties.

S.1 Components

The components of the **LMS** described here express the overall structure of the system.

S.1.1 Books Management

S.1.1.1 The Books Management component concerns the **Books** and includes **Books** description.

S.1.1.2 Books Management includes **Catalog** generation with the number of copies available for each **Book**, searching for **Books**, and displaying the list of **Books**.

S.1.1.3 A **Meta Book** is described by its title, author, **ISBN** number, number of copies, and number of available copies.

S.1.1.4 A **Book** is a copy of a **Meta Book** (an instance), with a copy number and an availability status.

S.1.1.5 A **Book** on hold is unavailable until the **Hold Duration** has expired or until the **Patron** who placed it on hold has canceled it.

S.1.2 Patrons Management

S.1.2.1 The Patrons Management component includes {patrons'} identification and description, with their first name, family name, ID number, address, and penalties.

S.1.2.2 The Patrons Management component includes the number of **Books** placed on hold and the number of borrowed **Books**.

S.1.2.3 A **Patron** with three penalties is removed from the **Library** and is not be able to subscribe for 1 year.

S.1.2.4 The Patrons Management component includes functions allowing **Patrons** to modify their personal information.

S.1.2.5 The Patrons Management component includes functions allowing **Librarians** to add penalties to **Patrons'** files.

S.1.3 Holds Management

S.1.3.1 The Holds Management component would handle the holds.

S.1.3.2 The Holds Management component includes functions to place **Books** on hold, cancel holds, check holds expirations, and generate daily sheets.

S.1.3.3 The Holds Management component would store information about which **Patron** has placed which **Book** on hold and the date of the **Holding**.

S.1.4 Checkouts Management

S.1.4.1 The Checkouts Management component would handle the checking out and returning of **Books**.

S.1.4.2 Checkouts Management includes functions for managing the borrowing and the return of books.

S.1.4.3 The Checkouts Management component would store information about which **Patron** has checked out which **Book** and when it is due to be returned.

S.2 Functionality

 We list here the functional and non-functional properties describing the behaviors of the system's components.

S.2.1 Functional Requirements for the LMS

S.2.1.1 Ability for **Librarians** to add and remove **Books** from the **Library**.
S.2.1.2 Ability for all users to search for **Books** in the **Library** by title, author, or **ISBN**.
S.2.1.3 Ability for **Patrons** to place hold on **Books**.
S.2.1.4 Ability for **Librarians** to enter check out and return of **Books**.
S.2.1.5 Ability for all users to display a list of all **Books** in the **Library**.
S.2.1.6 Ability for all users to retrieve information about **Library Patrons**, including their name and ID number.
S.2.1.7 Ability for **Librarians** to track which **Books** are currently checked out and when they are due to be returned.
S.2.1.8 For 6 months, weekly reminder emails for overdue users, with updated amount of fees.
S.2.1.9 Suspension emails to **Patrons** having the maximum number of penalties.
S.2.1.10 Radiation emails to 6 months overdue **Patrons**.
S.2.1.11 Ability to generate reports on **Library** usage, holds, and **Checkouts**.

S.2.2 Non-functional Requirements for the LMS

S.2.2.1 User-friendly interface for easy navigation and use
S.2.2.2 High performance and scalability to handle large amounts of data
S.2.2.3 Data security and protection to ensure the privacy and confidentiality of **Library Patrons** and their information
S.2.2.4 Compatibility with various operating systems and devices
S.2.2.5 Ability to handle multiple users and concurrent access to the system
S.2.2.6 Compliance with relevant laws and regulations regarding **Library** management and data privacy
S.2.2.7 Regular updates and maintenance to ensure the system remains functional and secure over time

S.3 Interfaces

This chapter lists user interfaces and program interfaces (APIs) handling the functionality and making them available.

S.3.1 Users should be able to access **LMS** from any device that has Internet-browsing capabilities and an Internet connection.

S.4 Detailed Usage Scenarios

- Here are some examples of interactions between the environment (or human users) and the system.
- These scenarios detail some functional properties and take into account the Environment properties described in **E.3**

S.4.1 Reserve_a_book

Name	Reserve_a_book
Scope	System
Level	Business summary
Primary actor	**Patron**
Context of use	A **Patron** wants to place hold on a **Book** so that the **Book** is reserved before he picks it up
Preconditions	The **Library** has a requested **Book** Patron is logged in to the **Library** system
Trigger	The **Patron** finds in a **Library Catalog** the **Book** he wants to borrow and requests the system to place a hold on this **Book**
Main success scenario	1. System validates that a hold can be placed 2. The system reserves a **Book** by the **Patron** 3. The system displays the confirmation that the hold is placed successfully 4. The system tags the starting date of the hold
Success guarantee	The **Book** is on hold by the **Patron**

Name	Reserve_a_book
Extensions	1A. The **Book** is checked out • The system denies placing hold on the **Book** • The system displays error message 1B. The **Book** is on hold by another **Patron** • The system denies placing hold on the **Book** • The system displays error message 1C. The **Patron** has five **Books** on hold • The system denies placing hold on the **Book** • The system displays error message 1D. The **Patron** has an **Overdue Checkout** • The system denies placing hold on the **Book** • The system displays Warning message
Stakeholders and interests	**Patron** (reserves a **Book**) **Librarian** (enforces adherence to **Library** policies)

S.4.2 Borrow_a_book

Name	Borrow_a_book
Scope	System

Name	Borrow_a_book
Level	Business summary
Primary actor	**Librarian**
Context of use	The **Patron** wants to check out a **Book**
Preconditions	The **Book** is available
Trigger	The **Patron** found in the library **Catalog** the **Book** he wants to borrow and requested successfully the system to place a hold on this **Book**

5.1 A Library Management System (LMS)

Name	Borrow_a_book
Main success Scenario	The system changes the **Book** status to borrowed The **Patron** checks out the **Book**. The **Patron** returns the **Book**
Success guarantee	The **Patron** has borrowed the **Book** and returned it within the checkout duration.

Name	Borrow_a_book
Extensions	1. The hold expires 　The system changes the hold status to expired and the **Book** becomes available 2. The **Patron** canceled the hold 　The **Book** status changes to available 3. The **Patron** does not return the **Book** within the maximum check out duration The **Book** status changes to overdue A penalty is added to the **Patron's** file The **Patron** returns the **Book**
Stakeholders and interests	**Patron** (borrows a **Book**), **Librarians**—register actions of borrowing and return

S.5 Prioritization

We choose to not classify behaviors, interfaces, and scenarios according to their degree of criticality, as all of them are equally important for this system.

S.6 Verification and Acceptance Criteria

In this last chapter of the System book, we specify the conditions under which an implementation will be deemed satisfactory. Verification and acceptance criteria for an online Library Management System (LMS) should ensure that the system meets its requirements and performs as expected.

All functional requirements such as "Librarians can add, edit, and delete books" or "patrons can search for books by title, author, ISBN," which are not repeated here, must be met for these verification purposes.

S.6.1 Verification Criteria for the LMS

S.6.1.1 The system responds to user actions within an acceptable time frame (search results within 2 s).
S.6.1.2 The system can handle concurrent users without significant performance degradation.
S.6.1.3 User data is encrypted and securely stored.
S.6.1.4 The system sends notifications for **Overdue Checkout** and due dates via email or SMS.
S.6.1.5 The user interface is intuitive and easy to navigate.

S.6.1.6 The system can scale to accommodate a growing number of users and library resources.

S.6.2 Acceptance Criteria for the LMS

S.6.2.1 All functional verification criteria are met.
S.6.2.2 Users from each user role (**Librarian**, **Patron**) have tested the system and confirmed it meets their needs.
S.6.2.3 Comprehensive user manuals and technical documentation are provided.
S.6.2.4 The system is successfully deployed in the production environment.
S.6.2.5 Support resources are available.

5.1.5 Project

The Project book describes all the constraints and expectations not about the system itself but about how to develop and produce it.

P.1 Roles and Personnel

We identified the main responsibilities in the **LMS** project: required project staff and their needed qualifications.

Project roles	Personnel
Project manager	Team principal
Testers	Library manager
Documenters	Systems engineers
Developers	Systems engineers

P.1.1 The project team includes a project manager and three systems engineers 100% dedicated to the project.
P.1.2 The team is composed of four students in software engineering.
P.1.3 The requirements analysis, software development, and testing are performed by the team member responsible for the specific software modules.
P.1.4 The team has to plan to test the product with the **Library** manager as a super user able to switch from one role to another one to ensure the correctness and safety of the developed software.

P.2 Imposed Technical Choices

A priori choices of specific tools, hardware, and languages are depicted below.

P.2.1 Users may access **LMS** from any device with Internet-browsing capabilities and an Internet connection.

5.1 A Library Management System (LMS)

P.2.2 Users must authenticate with their correct usernames and passwords to enter their online accounts and do actions.

P.2.3 The information of all users, **Books**, and **Library** must be stored in a database accessible by the system.

P.3 Schedule and Milestones

Following the Minimum Requirements Outcome Principle, we established a list of tasks to be carried out and their scheduling.

P.3.1 The project should provide a first prototype (v.1) on May 30, 2024.

P.3.2 A second milestone is planned for a v.2 with the remaining features, in May 1, 2025.

P.4 Tasks and Deliverables

Details of individual tasks listed under **P.3** and their expected outcomes are expressed in this chapter.

P.4.1 The tasks and deliverables are listed in the Gantt diagram provided in Appendix TBD.

P.5 Required Technology Elements

In this chapter, we give external systems that seem necessary for building the system, but the choice of the tool is open to the developers.

P.5.1 MongoDB for the database.

P.5.2 JavaScript for building the Web application.

P.5.3 Maven for the project management.

P.5.4 The Login management module is not dedicated to a **Library** and must be an external module added to the **LMS**.

P.6 Risks and Mitigation Analysis

We have not identified any potential obstacles to meeting the schedule of **P.4** and so give no measure for adapting the plan.

P.7 Requirements Process and Report

We describe the requirements process based on the PEGS approach.

P.7.1 The project utilizes the PEGS approach to requirements. Requirements are developed incrementally and allocated to one of the four books.

P.7.2 The process is conducted in an agile way.

P.7.3 The team leader is the scrum master and PO Proxy.

P.7.4 The PO is a **Library** manager.
P.7.5 During the implementation phase, whenever change or refinement of the requirements is detected, it should be carefully documented and confirmed with the stakeholders.

5.2 A Book on Requirements

5.2.1 Context

This case study constitutes the requirements documentation for this **companion book**. It follows the method presented in **The Handbook**, as an attempt to illustrate PEGS's general purpose and as a tribute to one of the favorite Bertrand Meyer's practices.

It uses the AsciiDoc template available on the **The Handbook's Companion Website**, where the reader will also find the full version of the requirements document.

In the following, we illustrate and discuss some of our choices, hesitations, and the benefit of using PEGS, even for developing a non-software product.

This case study is very special because it is biased, as the requirements author was also the system's developer. Nevertheless, it shows the benefit of having a well-organized set of requirements for developing any new project.

5.2.2 Changelog

As the reader can see in the following extract from the changelog, the updates of the project artifacts (in our case, some of the Standard Plan chapter's titles) or the late application of good principles are precisely traced.

Example 2 Extract of the Changelog

Version	Date	Comment
1.0	2021-02-01	Initial draft by **J.-M. Bruel**
1.1	2021-02-08	Organization in separate books' files, by **J.-M. Bruel**
1.2	2021-02-21	Writing of the Process book, by **J.-M. Bruel**

Version	Date	Comment
1.2.1	2021-02-29	Minor improvements of verification rules, by **J.-M. Bruel**
1.2.2	2021-04-16	Minor improvements of goals, by **J.-M. Bruel**
1.2.3	2023-08-02	Add an example of business constraint and its rationale in E.3, by **J.-M. Bruel**
1.2.4	2023-08-24	Add an example of Assumption in E.4, and add Minimum Outcome Principle feature, by **J.-M. Bruel**

Here is an even stronger policy, appplied at **McMaster University**, in their 2023 Requirements Engineering course:

Control Information

Version	Delivery		Feedback	
	Deadline	Delivered	Received	Integrated
V1	15/08/2023	13/08/2023		
V2				
V3				

Fig. 5.1 Control information of the Requirements Documentation at **McMaster University**

They even use one for each Book:

Control Information

Table 1. ATCO Eats — Versionning Information — Goal Book

Section	Version	Lead	Delivered on	Reviewer	Approved on
G.1	1	GPT-3.5	M1		
G.2	1	GPT-3.5	M1		

Fig. 5.2 Control information of the Goals book

Version	Date	Comment
1.2.5	2023-08-25	Fix Standard plan updates, by **J.-M. Bruel**
1.2.6	2023-08-27	Add Scenarios and authors, by **J.-M. Bruel**

The author of the changes (as well as a quick way to contact him or her) is important.

 Here is an even stronger policy, applied at **McMaster University**, in their 2023 Requirements Engineering course (Fig. 5.1):
They even use one for each Book (Fig. 5.2):

5.2.3 Goals Book

Front Matter

Apart from the table of contents[2], we have not used any other of the recommended information for front matter:

- Title (whether or not on a separate title page)
- Date of current publication and revision history
- Copyright notice, distribution information, restrictions on distribution
- Approval information

---

[2] Not shown in this chapter but in the full version

We nevertheless show how to do so in the source of the document (in AsciiDoc) for future improvement and for the readers who would like to use it as teaching material.

Numbering Requirements

We systematically numbered the requirements and referred to any glossary entry when writing the requirements.

The input format (**AsciiDoc**) allows the definition of specific numbering and referencing rules.

Here is the one used in this case study:

```
//---- Requirement
[[g1-mainGoal]]       ①
^`G.1.{counter:comp-g1}`^   ②
The main purpose of the {companion} is to complement the {Handbook}
by providing useful additional material, examples, templates, and
full {method} use cases.   ③
//----
```

An example of "source code" requirement

① Anchor definition (for potential referencing).

② Incrementation of the chapter's specific counter. The addition of deletion of a requirement renumbers automatically all the following ones.

③ Use of variables to reference Glossary entries or URLs.

 See the corresponding output in the **G.1 chapter**.

Goals Book Requirements

G.1 Context and Overall Objective

> G.1.1 The main purpose of the **companion book** is to complement **The Handbook** by providing useful additional material, examples, templates, and full PEGS use cases.
> ⊗ No corresponding artifact required.

G.2 Current Situation

> G.2.1 The only available material at the beginning of the project is the published **The Handbook**.
> ⊗ No corresponding artifact required.

G.3 Expected Benefits

G.3.1 **Readers** of the **companion book** should be able to find some templates for the requirements' book structure.
⊘ Corresponding Artifact: **Appendix E**

 This Goal requirement is testable (by checking the presence of such a template); to demonstrate that it is satisfied, we refer to the corresponding artifact, which happens to be one of the chapters of this companion book.

G.4 Functionality Overview

G.4.1 The *system under development* in this specification is an unusual one: a book! This requirements document will serve as one of the case studies for the **companion book**.
⊘ Corresponding Artifact: Sect. 5.2

G.5 High-Level Usage Scenarios

G.5.1 The main target usage of the **companion book** is to practice **The Handbook** principles.
⊗ No corresponding artifact required.

G.5.2 An expected usage of the **companion book** is for Requirements Engineering courses teachers to get materials for their class.
⊗ No corresponding artifact is required.

G.6 Limitations and Exclusions

⚠ Nothing available at this point (Tables 5.1 and 5.2)

 The template defines an `emptysec` variable so that the same text appears throughout the empty chapters. This can be useful in the initial stages of the writing or for students' templates, for example. It also allowed us to easily implement the *Minimum Requirements Outcome Principle* when AsciiDoc is the input language for requirements writing.
Here is its definition in the AsciiDoc template:

```
:emptysec:   icon:warning[]   Nothing   available   at
this point.
```

Table 5.1 Target side stakeholders

Stakeholder	Category	Comment
Springer	Legal department	In charge of the edition of the **companion book**
Readers of **The Handbook**	User	Readers of the main **The Handbook** that might need additional information about the method
Readers of the **companion book**	User	Persons reading the **companion book** who might not have access to the main **The Handbook**

Table 5.2 Production side stakeholders

Stakeholder	Category	Comment
Author of the Handbook	Domain Expert	Bertrand Meyer, author of **The Handbook**, and main evaluator of the **companion book**
Leader of the companion book	Project Manager	**J.-M. Bruel**, effort leader of the **companion book**
Authors of the companion book	Developers	**J.-M. Bruel**, **Sophie Ebersold**, and **Mariya Naumcheva**, authors of the **companion book**

> We omit the other empty chapters in the remaining sections of this case study presentation. This one was mentioned to illustrate how to deal with those empty chapters.

G.7 Stakeholders and Requirements Sources

> G.7.1 Here is a non-exhaustive list of the stakeholders.
> ⊗ No corresponding artifact is required.

> G.7.2 Most of the requirements come from **The Handbook**.
> ⊗ No corresponding artifact is required.

5.2.4 Environment Book

E.1 Glossary

This section defines the domain-specific terms used in this document. It also lists the icons used in this document.

5.2 A Book on Requirements

 ⊗ All the requirements elements of this chapter, by definition, do not require any corresponding artifact.

E.1.1 Terms

Companion Book
The *system* to be developed: the companion book of **The Handbook** Current version available at https://formalrequirements.github.io/companionRequirements

The Handbook
The book, entitled *Handbook of Requirements and Business Analysis*, written by Bertrand Meyer (see the Springer link about **The Handbook**), for which the **companion book** serves as complementary material.

E.1.2 Icons

Here is the list of significations for the icons used when tracing the corresponding artifacts (Table 5.3):

E.3 Constraints

E.3.1 The **companion book** should itself apply the method described in **The Handbook**.
⊗ No corresponding artifact required.

E.3.2 The **companion book** should reach at least 160–170 pages.
⊘ Corresponding artifact: Current page count is 219.

E.3.3 The rationale for requirement **E.3.2** is: in order to have a sufficient distinction from the **SpringerBriefs**.

 This requirement illustrates how to refer to another one.
Here is an excerpt of the AsciiDoc source of the requirement:

```
The rationale for requirement <<e3-pages,E.3.{e3-pages}>> is...
```

| | No corresponding artifact is required. |

Table 5.3 Icons signification

Icon	Signification
⊘	A precisely referenced artifact satisfying the requirement just expressed
⊗	A kind of requirement that do not imply any artifact to trace
🐞	No corresponding artifact yet (requirement not yet satisfied)
💡	We have considered that a list of terms is one requirement only; hence, we have numbered the list accordingly.

E.4 Assumptions

> E.4.1 The **companion book** will be reviewed by the author of **The Handbook**).
> 🐞 Corresponding artifact: not yet available.

5.2.5 Project Book

P.1 Roles and Personnel

> P.1.1 Here are the only considered roles for the production of the **companion book**:
> - Leader: the person in charge of leading and organizing the writing effort
> - Writers: the persons contributing to the writing effort
> - Reviewers: the persons in charge of reviewing the **companion book**
>
> ⊗ No corresponding artifact is required.

> P.1.2 Here are the only identified people involved in the development of the **companion book**:
> - Leader: The writing effort of the **companion book** is under the responsibility of **J.-M. Bruel**.
> - Writers: In addition to **J.-M. Bruel**, the following are also involved: **Sophie Ebersold**, **Mariya Naumcheva**, Alexandr Naumchev, and Florian Galinier.
> - Reviewers: In addition to **Bertrand Meyer**, author of **The Handbook**, some reviewers will be found among early adopters of **The Handbook**.
>
> ▼ *TBD*
> **Author**
>   J.-M. Bruel

5.2 A Book on Requirements

Date
  2023-02-21
Deadline
  June
Importance
  serious
Needs
  ☐ stakeholders to ask
  ☐ documentation to consider
  ☑ management decision (by **Bertrand Meyer**)
  ⊗ No corresponding artifact required

 This requirement illustrates how to describe the important information about the *To be Determined*.
In our AsciiDoc context, we are using the benefit of the `collapsible` attribute. The above text (the printed version) is fully defined, but the HTML version, illustrated in the following figure, is collapsed (Fig. 5.3).

P.2 Imposed Technical Choices

P.2.1   The **companion book** should be written in English.
⊘ See for yourself!

P.2.2   The **companion book** should be written in one of the compatible inputs of the publisher, Springer.
🐞 Requirement not yet satisfied

Fig. 5.3 HTML (collapsed) version of a To Be Determined

P.3 Schedule and Milestones

^{P.3.1} The expected date of the **companion book** is the end of June.
🜛 Deadline missed

P.4 Tasks and Deliverables

^{P.4.1} The tasks are managed through the use of a collaborative repository.
⊘ Corresponding artifact: https://github.com/FormalRequirements/requirements-handbook

P.7 Requirements Process and Report

^{P.7.1} The production of the **companion book** will not follow a particular requirements process.
⊗ No corresponding artifact required

> *Back matter*
> **TBD list**
> - **P.1.2**.

5.2.6 System Book

The "system" under development in this case study is the companion book you are reading. Hence, the System Book has not been written with the same application as the others.

S.1 Components

^{S.1.1} The components of the **companion book** initially identified are the following:

- ^{S.1.1.1} An overview of the PEGS method
- ^{S.1.1.2} At least one case study
- ^{S.1.1.3} At least one book template

⊘ Corresponding artifact are Chaps. 4 and 5 and **Appendix E** (for, respectively, S.1.1.1, S.1.1.2, and S.1.1.3).

5.2 A Book on Requirements

Back Matter

As for the front matter, we have not used any other recommended information for the back matter, apart from a recap list of *To-Be-Determined* tasks.

Back matter
TBD list
- [p1-persons]

5.2.7 Traceability Matrix

One way to enforce the quality of the development is to check whether each requirement has some sort of implementation (at least one, in the form of a concrete artifact or a measurable result) and vice versa if each key element of the system (e.g., component, function) corresponds to at least one requirement. Such traceability links are easily represented through a traceability matrix, as illustrated for this companion book in Table 5.4.

In the following table, when the Checking column is OK (⊘), the corresponding Implementation column contains the reference to the corresponding artifact. When it is not OK (⊗), it explains why there is no corresponding artifact.

Another interesting coverage evaluation is the reverse matrix, which shows, for each chapter (or even section), the corresponding requirement(s) it fulfills.

As the case study was only illustrative, we have not updated the companion book requirements while improving the book with more targets, features, and chapters. Hence, this matrix is provided only for some obvious chapters in the **following matrix** as an illustration (Table 5.5).

Table 5.4 Traceability matrix between the requirements and some parts of the book

Req #	Checking	Implementation
G.1.1	⊗	Goal requirement: tell us if it is satisfied (Satisfied from the satisfaction of **S.1.1.1**, **S.1.1.2**, and **S.1.1.3**, from our point of view)
G.2.1	⊗	Assumption (about **The Handbook** itself)
G.3.1	⊘	**Appendix E**
G.4.1	⊘	Section 5.2
G.5.1	⊗	Goal requirement: tell us if it is satisfied
G.5.2	⊗	But see the list of courses in http://requirements.university
G.7.1	⊗	Meta requirement: no implementation
G.7.2	⊗	Justification requirement: no implementation
E.1.1	⊗	Definitions: no implementation
E.1.2	⊗	Definitions: no implementation
E.3.1	⊗	You have to trust us on this one

(continued)

Table 5.4 (continued)

Req #	Checking	Implementation
E.3.2	⊘	`page-count = 219`
E.3.3	⊗	`Justification` requirement: no implementation
E.4.1	⊗	You have to trust us on this one
P.1.1	⊗	Definitions: no implementation
P.1.2	⊗	Definitions: no implementation
P.2.1	⊘	This one is tricky to trace
P.2.2	⊘	See the editor of this book (should say "Springer")
P.3.1	🔥	We missed the initial deadline
P.4.1	⊘	Private repo: https://github.com/FormalRequirements/requirements-handbook
P.7.1	⊘	The process is described in this chapter
S.1.1.1	⊘	Chapter 2
S.1.1.2	⊘	Chapter 5
S.1.1.3	⊘	**Appendix E**

Table 5.5 Traceability matrix between some parts of the book and the requirements

Section #	Corresponding req #
Chapter 2	**S.1.1.1** and **G1.1**
Chapter 5	**S.1.1.2** and **G1.1**
Appendix E	**S.1.1.3** and **G1.3**
…	…

5.3 The Roborace

5.3.1 Context

To test and evaluate the PEGS approach, we have applied it to a real-world software project—the Roborace. Roborace is a championship between autonomous cars where competing teams must develop autonomous driving software. We have collaborated with one of the teams participating in the championship to elicit and document requirements according to the PEGS approach.

This chapter presents an excerpt from the Roborace case study. The extended version of this case study is available on the **companion website**.

5.3.2 Goals Book

As the project started with goals and feasibility assessment, we started documenting requirements with the Goals book. Although there are no restrictions on the order in which the sections of the PEGS template are completed, it is safe to say that the Goals book should be close to completion before proceeding to the other books, with few exceptions. In the Roborace project, we set up an elicitation meeting to understand the project context and fix project goals and limitations. The sections of the Goals book served as a canvas for the meeting structure.

G.1 Context and Overall Objective

 This section provides a bird's-eye overview of the project. We numbered each paragraph as a separate subsection so that it could be easily referenced when needed.

G.1.1 Roborace is a global championship between autonomous cars that allows testing driverless technology in the extreme conditions of competition. The participating teams get access to a **race car** called **Devbot 2.0** and simulation facilities and have to develop the software to drive Devbot 2.0 in racing conditions. The teams are not allowed to modify the hardware.

G.1.2 The Roborace provides facilities for driverless technology development and testing. The **SIT Acronis** team aims to use this opportunity to develop a software that can be licensed and sold.

G.1.3 The current project focuses on developing the software for **Devbot 2.0**.

G.2 Current Situation

 This section describes the current state of affairs concerning software development.

G.2.1 Roborace develops and maintains the hardware. The vehicle is fully ready for autonomous racing, and technical specifications are provided to the **SIT Acronis** team.

G.2.2 Initially, Roborace partially provides the software (such as the localization module), and the performance requirements are moderate (limited max speed, no physical competition with the other vehicles, etc.). Gradually, the teams participating in racing competitions should transfer to their software and be able to handle more sophisticated tasks, such as obstacle avoidance, overtaking maneuvers, high-speed racing, and localization without GNSS.

G.3 Expected Benefits

 The specifics of the Roborace project are that the project team's goal is not to improve current processes but to create a technology that can be licensed and sold. We reflect this aspect in the project's goals:

G.3.1 Promotion of **SIT** as the pioneer of driverless racing.
G.3.2 Revenue from the sales of the developed software.
G.3.3 Revenue from sponsorship contracts.

 Even though this formulation of the project goals diverges from their definition in the Handbook as "new processes, or improvement to existing processes, made possible by the project's results," it best helps to keep the project focused: the decisions made along the project must ultimately serve the satisfaction of these goals.

G.4 Functionality Overview

Sections **G.4—Functionality Overview** and **G.5—High-Level Usage Scenarios**, at first sight, seem to overlap since scenarios often capture functional requirements, especially in agile projects. Nevertheless, in the Roborace project, these sections cover completely different aspects of the system. Section G.4 covers key functions of the developed software, whereas Section G.5 describes the main scenarios of interacting with the system, not only its software part. The reason is that scenarios are a way to describe expected system behaviors in a language understandable by all project stakeholders. Further analysis is required to extract software functionality from scenarios.

This section contains very-high-level description of system functionality, which will be further refined in the System book.

G.4.1 The system shall enable the **Devbot 2.0** to drive autonomously, without a human pilot. For accomplishing this global task, the system shall have the following functionalities:

G.4.1.1 Calculate the optimal path and velocity profile for a given racetrack
G.4.1.2 Locate the race car on a map of a racetrack
G.4.1.3 Calculate local path
G.4.1.4 Control and stabilize the **Devbot 2.0** in real-time
G.4.1.5 Identify and track obstacles
G.4.1.6 Calculate the optimal race strategy
G.4.1.7 Ensure safe operation of **Devbot 2.0** (avoid collisions and track departure)

G.5 High-Level Usage Scenarios

Scenarios are formulated in the language of system users and can serve as a "unit of delivery." However, scenarios cannot completely cover the software functionality in systems with complex business logic, such as the Roborace software. They may serve project planning, elicitation, and testing purposes, yet additional techniques are required to describe business logic and constraints on software functionality. We discovered a list of key use cases during the first elicitation meeting without additional details. To understand the project goals and scope, we explore the basic flow of the two use cases with the highest priority for the project. Further detailization of use cases occurs during the project and should be documented in the Systems book.

G.5.1 **Calculate raceline**. The system shall calculate an optimal raceline (trajectory and speed) for a given 2D map of a racetrack.

G.5.2 **Race without obstacles**. The system shall autonomously drive a Devbot on a racetrack for a given number of laps and then stop it.

Basic flow of the use case:

- Human pilot positions **Devbot 2.0** behind a starting line and leaves.
- The Race Control Unit sends a **green flag** to the system.
- The race car pilot turns on the race mode in a system.
- The system drives **Devbot 2.0** a given number of laps and performs a **safe stop** after crossing the starting line.

G.5.3 **Update speed limit**. The system shall update speed limit upon request.
G.5.4 **Race with virtual static obstacles**. Demonstrate the fastest total time, taking into account bonus and penalty time.
G.5.5 **Race with virtual dynamic obstacles**. Demonstrate the fastest total time, taking into account bonus and penalty time.
G.5.6 **Perform an emergency stop**. Perform an emergency stop upon request.
G.5.7 **Perform a safe stop**. Perform a **safe stop** upon request.

Basic flow of the use case:

- The system receives a request to perform a safe stop.
- The system recalculates the local trajectory to meet the safe deceleration limit.
- The race car gradually stops following the recalculated trajectory.

G.6 Limitations and Exclusions

We found this section very useful for clearly defining project boundaries. At the same time, some of the limitations could not be identified during the first elicitation meeting and required exploring the subject domain and consulting project stakeholders. For example, limitation G.6.1 comes from the Roborace team and thus could be clearly identified at the very beginning of the project. Limitations G.6.2 to G.6.4, however, required discussions with domain experts and assessing project resources.

G.6.1 Hardware modifications are outside the scope of the project, which concerns solely software production. Roborace management performs hardware modifications, if any, and communicates them to the **SIT Acronis** Team as part of future mission rules.
G.6.2 The system does not take into account weather conditions (wind, temperature, precipitation).
G.6.3 The system does not take into account **tire degradation, tire wear**, and other factors affecting tire friction.
G.6.4 The system does not utilize **torque vectoring**.

Some of the terms in G.4 contain hyperlinks. The links lead to the corresponding entries in the glossary (**E.1**).

G.7 Stakeholders and Requirements Sources

We relied on the table of potential stakeholder classes provided in the requirements handbook for stakeholder analysis. We describe each of the stakeholder groups as a separate requirement.

G.7.1 **Users**. The core users of the systems are **Devbot 2.0** operators. In the current project, they are all **SIT Acronis** team members and participate in software development.
G.7.2 **Subject-Matter Experts**. SMEs are a source of information about various aspects of racing and autonomous driving.

G.7.3 **Legal department**. Since the project aims to license and sell software, legal assistance is required to address intellectual property issues.

The Roborace project is a research project since it involves solving tasks on the edge of driverless technology. Consequently, related work plays an important role in understanding requirements. We collected the related work in a separate folder and referenced it in section G.7.8. Another important source of requirements is technical documentation, including the specification of interfaced systems and technical regulations of the Roborace championship.

G.7.8 **Other requirements sources**. This section serves as a collection of links to requirements sources other than those of the stakeholders.

We do not disclose the documents, provided by the Roborace, since they are not intended for public use.

- G.7.8.1 Publications made by university-based teams participating in the Roborace competition.
- G.7.8.2 Technical specification provided by the Roborace.
- G.7.8.3 Mission rules:
- G.7.8.3.1 Mission 1 rules
- G.7.8.3.2 Mission 1.1 rules
- G.7.8.3.3 Mission 2 rules
- G.7.8.4 Technical specification of the Devbot's sensors and APIs that they provide
- G.7.8.5 Regulatory documents on autonomous driving

5.3.3 Environment

Unlike the Goals book, which is mostly completed in a single effort, the other books are developed in iterations. The major part of the Environment book precedes the specification of the System book because environment properties and constraints affect the requirements. At the same time, the glossary is subject to change and accumulates all new terms that come up during the project.

E.1 Glossary

A glossary is a constantly updated body of knowledge about domain-specific terms. Our initial approach to the glossary was adding all domain-specific terms we encountered during domain knowledge acquisition. The resulting glossary, however, included many terms that never appeared in the requirements document, while many used terms needed to be included. So we switched to another approach for selecting glossary entries: we added to the glossary any term appearing in requirements that could be interpreted in more than one way. Further on, we added bookmarks to glossary entries on each appearance of such terms.

In the Glossary, we diverge from the PEGS approach that recommends numbering each section of the document. Glossary entries are not numbered since they are easier to reference by a hyperlink or a name of an entry.

As for other sub-sections of this section, this glossary is only an excerpt (see the **companion website** for the full version).

Car
A synonym to a **race car** and **Devbot 2.0**.

Curb
Flat curbstones lining the corners or chicanes of a **racetrack**. They are often painted red and white and are intended to prevent unauthorized shortcuts and keep the racers safely on the **racetrack**.

Devbot 2.0
The all-electric vehicle used for Roborace Seasons Alpha and Beta, a rear-wheel drive car that can be piloted by a human or AI driver.

Did Not Finish (DNF)
A run is scored as a DNF when a portion of the course was not completed or when a car fails on course.

Drivable area
The area where a self-driving vehicle can safely operate.

Ego vehicle
A vehicle that contains the **sensors** that perceive the environment around the vehicle.

Electronic control unit (ECU)
An embedded unit in the vehicle that controls one or more electrical systems, such as the engine control unit or the human-machine interface.

Emergency stop
A stop applying emergency brake (maximum allowed deceleration rate).

Event
A **practice session** or a **race** in the Roborace Championship Calendar.

Ghost car
A dynamic virtual obstacle that simulates a competing car.

Gizmo
A virtual obstacle in a **Metaverse**.

GNSS data
Positioning information provided by satellite-based positioning systems in real time.

Lidar
A **sensor** used for creating 2D or 3D representation of the surveyed environment by emitting pulsed laser lights and processing their reflections.

The local trajectory
The optimal trajectory to follow a global reference trajectory (a **raceline**) while avoiding **obstacles** in a smooth way.

Loot
A static virtual **obstacle** that brings bonuses when collected.

Metaverse
Mixed reality racing format, in which cars race against virtual objects appearing on the actual **racetrack**.

Mission
A series of **races** (usually two races over one weekend) that follow the same rules.

Obstacle
A physical or virtual object on a **drivable area** of a **racetrack**. Virtual obstacles are introduced in the Roborace **Metaverse**.

Pilot
A person that remotely operates the **Devbot 2.0** on a **racetrack**.

Pit
An area of a **racetrack** where the backup personnel for the **race car** is located.

Pitlane
A lane adjacent (usually on the inner curve) to a **racetrack** where the competing teams' garages are situated.

Pose
Position and orientation of a **race car**.

Position
State of the car in the **reference coordinate system**.

Practice session
A driving session with **Devbot 2.0** on a physical **racetrack**, aimed to test software, adjust settings, and test the true pace of the car.

Race
A competition between autonomous **race cars**. The race usually takes up to several hours and is a part of a **mission**.

Race car
A synonym for **Devbot 2.0**.

Race operator
A member of the SIT team who remotely operates the Roborace **event**.

Raceline
The optimal path around a **racetrack** considering given acceleration and velocity constraints.

Racetrack
A circular road with a hard surface built for racing of the vehicles.

Race control unit (RCU)
Roborace representatives who are responsible for monitoring and supervising the **practice sessions** and the **race**.

Rules
A set of goals and limitations that Roborace competing teams must follow for a given **mission**.

Safe stop
A stop applying comfort deceleration rate.

Sensor
A device that receives input from the environment and converts it into digital data.

SIT
Schaffhausen Institute of Technology, our client for the Roborace at the time of writing these requirements.

Starting line
A line orthogonal to the **racetrack's bounding lines**. A **race car** starts a **race** behind the **starting line** and finishes a race after crossing the **starting line**.

Tire degradation
An overall decrease in performance of the tires due to an imbalance of temperature.

Tire wear
Physical wearing out of a tire over time and use.

Torque vectoring
Controlling the distribution of torque between individual wheels.

Velocity profile
A sequence of velocities along the trajectory (Fig. 5.4).

E.2 Components

E.2.1 Roborace management.

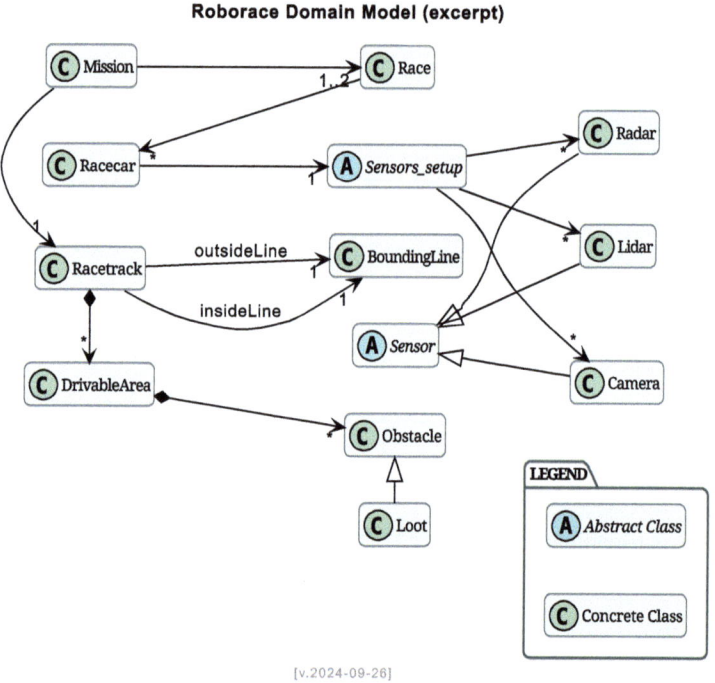

Fig. 5.4 Exerpt of the Roborace Domain Model

5.3 The Roborace

E.2.2 The components of the **racetrack** relevant to the present requirements are:

- E.2.2.1 **Racetrack surface.**
- E.2.2.2 **Racetrack map.**

E.2.3 **Race Control Unit** may interfere with a **race car's** operation by issuing one among the following flags, with their respective meanings:

- E.2.3.1 Green flag: the **race car** can race without any additional restrictions.
- E.2.3.2 Yellow flag: the **race car** must move in a safe mode (with restricted speed and acceleration). Overtaking not allowed.
- E.2.3.3 Red flag: the **race car** must perform an **emergency stop**.

E.2.4 The effect of a race car hitting an obstacle differs for **virtual** and **physical** obstacle:

- E.2.4.1 For a virtual **obstacle**, the only effect is a to impose on the car a bonus or a penalty as specified in the mission **rules**.
- E.2.4.2 For a physical **obstacle**, the effects are one or more of the following:
  - E.2.4.2.1 Damage to the **race car**.
  - E.2.4.2.2 Change to its trajectory.
  - E.2.4.2.3 Change to its velocity.
  - E.2.4.2.4 Hurting the **obstacle** if it is a person or an animal.

E.2.5 **Interfaces from the environment to the system**:

E.2.5.1 Roborace provides **localization data** for each event. Definition of the outputs provided to teams is located in a separate document.
E.2.5.2 **Safety module**'s software is provided by the Roborace.
E.2.5.3 Specifications of the interfaces provided by the **Devbot's sensors** are stored in a dedicated folder.

E.3 Constraints

E.3.1 Constraints on the Project

E.3.1.1 The team has very limited access to **Devbot 2.0** for testing purposes. Testing shall mostly rely on simulation facilities.
E.3.1.2 Project milestones are tied to the dates of Roborace races. Consequently, the deadlines for achieving targets of every mission are strict and cannot be postponed.
E.3.1.3 The team must submit the software for homologation by Roborace no later than 10 days before the event.

E.3.1.4 Software must be tested and verified before scheduling on-track testing session.
E.3.1.5 All personnel must receive e-safety training.

E.3.2 Constraints on the System

E.3.1.1 **Devbot 2.0** shall not cross the racetrack's bounding lines.
Source: 2nd interview
E.3.1.2 **Devbot 2.0** shall not accelerate and brake at the same moment.
Source: 2nd interview (engineering decision)
E.3.1.3 **Devbot 2.0** shall not drive on the **curbs**.
Source: 2nd interview
E.3.1.4 A system may receive a speed limit during the race and shall react accordingly. (business rule)
E.3.1.5 The speed of **Devbot 2.0** must never exceed the speed limit imposed by the **event**'s rules.
E.3.1.6 The acceleration of **Devbot 2.0** must never exceed the acceleration limit imposed by the Roborace.
Source: 2nd interview (business rule)

E.4 Assumptions

E.4.1 If there is no wheel slipping, a car is moving toward its heading direction.
E.4.2 The measured vehicle's speed equals to actual vehicle's speed with an accuracy 1 kph.
Source: 2nd interview
E.4.3 The estimated vehicle's pose equals to actual vehicle's pose with an accuracy 10 cm.
E.4.4 The racetrack surface is clean and in good conditions.
E.4.5 The racetrack surface is not slippery.
E.4.6 The **Devbot 2.0's** sensors do not fail during the race.
E.4.7 During the events, the Internet bandwidth and speed are sufficient for running the software.
E.4.8 The localization data is provided during the race in real time.
Source: 2nd interview
E.4.9 The track 2D map is provided before the race.
Source: 2nd interview
E.4.10 Racetrack is a closed loop.
E.4.11 Raceline is a closed loop.
E.4.12 Dynamic virtual obstacles move in the racing direction.
Source: 2nd interview

E.5 Effects

E.5.1 Currently the software is checked by the Roborace team before each competition. When the system is fully implemented, this process might change.

E.5.2 When path planning is successfully implemented, the teams will no longer receive high-precision localization data from Roborace.

E.5.3 The implementation of fully autonomous racing vehicles will lead to a redesign of the racing championship, as the racers' personalities play an important role in it. These changes are out of scope of this project.

E.6 Invariants

E.6.1 **Devbot 2.0** moves in autonomous mode only within racetrack limits.

5.3.4 System

The System book contains detailed requirements for the system's functionality. Since software is often developed in iterations, the level of detail can be substantially different for various system components. The requirements can be added, refined, or changed with each iteration. It is important to document and track those changes.

S.1 Components

The first iteration of developing system requirements focused on identifying system components and their responsibilities. **Devbot 2.0** is a cyber-physical system with software and hardware components. Due to the nature of the project, we focus only on software components or modules. Sensors and actuators serve as **interfaces** between the developed software and the world: sensors provide input data, and actuators receive output data from the system and transform it into respective actions. We thus list sensors and actuators as environment rather than system components.

S.1.1 **Planning module** is responsible for behavior and motion planning.

S.1.2 **Perception module** is responsible for obstacle detection, fusion, and situation prediction.

S.1.3 **Mapping and Localization module** is responsible for creating detailed representation of the environment and determining where on the map the vehicle is situated.

S.1.4 **Control module** is responsible for creating control command for steering, throttle, and brake actuators.

S.2 Functionality

The subsections in S.2 correspond to the subsections of S.1, but instead of a brief description, they provide a detailed list of requirements. As discussed above, the requirements listed in S.2 are subject to evolution over the project's development.

In the Roborace project, analysis of use cases (S.3) precedes documenting the requirements for functionality (S.2). The list of software requirements is elicited as a result of the analysis of the autonomous driving domain and the use cases. In some projects, the order may be reversed: first, produce the functional requirements, and second, elicit scenarios to test whether all requirements are covered.

S.2.1 Planning Module

Documenting this section involves analyzing the use cases and extracting the functionality of the system modules required for implementing the elicited scenarios.

S.2.1.1 Planning Module shall calculate the optimal **raceline** (trajectory and velocity profile) for a given **racetrack**.

S.2.1.1.1 At every position on a raceline, the speed in the velocity profile shall not exceed the speed limit.

S.2.1.1.2 Note1: Global raceline is calculated in offline mode, before the Roborace event start.

S.2.1.1.3 Note2: Various approaches for raceline calculation shall be explored and compared.

S.2.1.2 The planning module shall calculate the optimal maneuver to bypass an obstacle on a racetrack.

S.2.1.3 The planning module shall calculate the optimal local trajectory based on a global plan and current state of a **race car**.

S.2.1.3.1 The local trajectory shall be updated with the frequency of 10 Hz.

S.2.1.3.2 The local trajectory shall cover 100 future steps of the trajectory.

S.2.1.3.3 The local trajectory, if diverges from global trajectory due to encountering obstacles, shall merge with the global trajectory as soon as the obstacle is passed.

S.2.1.4 The planning module shall monitor the completion of the driving task (number of laps completed vs. target number of laps).

S.2.1.5 The planning module shall update state of the **race car** (standing still, racing, driving, emergency) according to the racing situation.

S.2.1.5.1 A **race car** is in a "standing still" mode if it is not moving, and no control commands (brake, steering, throttle) are applied.

S.2.1.6 The planning module shall calculate the optimal strategy of avoiding obstacles and collecting bonuses, which depends on the penalties and bonuses for the aforementioned actions.

S.2.1.7 When the system receives a **safe stop** request, the velocity profile of the calculated trajectory shall be updated so that the vehicle stops with a 1 m/s^2 deceleration.

S.2.1.8 When the system receives a **safe stop** request, the velocity profile of the calculated trajectory shall be updated so that the vehicle stops with an emergency brake deceleration.

S.2.6 Non-functional Requirements

We generally aimed to document non-functional requirements for each software component. Nevertheless, some non-functional requirements pertain to the system as a whole rather than a separate module. We list those requirements in this section.

S.2.6.1 The system response time must be under 600 ms.

S.3 Interfaces

This section answers two questions:
1. What interface does the system provide to its users?
2. What interface does the system provide to other systems?

Detailing interfaces is a task of system design. In section S.3, we list high-level requirements for the system interfaces.

S.3.1 The system will be run by a **race car pilot** on a laptop.
S.3.2 The system shall transmit the racing data to the Race Control Unit by V2X protocol.
S.3.3 The system shall send commands to actuators according to their specifications.

S.4 Detailed Usage Scenarios

The scenario specifications in this section are developed iteratively based on the priority of the scenarios. The scenarios with the highest priority are listed in **prioritization**. As an example, we list two use cases in a tabular form.

S.4.2 **Race without obstacles** (Table 5.6).
S.4.4 **Race with virtual static obstacles**. Demonstrate the fastest total time, taking into account bonus and penalty time (Table 5.7).

S.5 Prioritization

Different approaches could be applied to prioritize the requirements. Since the project team applies the agile project management approach, we prioritize the scenarios (listed in S.4) rather than individual requirements (listed in S.3). We list only the use cases with the highest priority and do not prioritize the remaining one, since due to the nature of the championship, the prioritization constantly evolves.

S.5.1 Due to the nature of the Roborace competition, requirements prioritization is subject to change according to the rules and goals of the upcoming Roborace events.
S.5.2 Scenarios with the highest priority:

- S.5.2.1 Race without obstacles
- S.5.2.2 Race with virtual static obstacles
- S.5.2.3 Perform an emergency stop
- S.5.2.4 Perform a **safe stop**

Table 5.6 Use Case 2. Single race without obstacles

Name	Single_race_no_obstacles
Scope	System
Level	Business summary
Primary actor	**Race car pilot**
Context of use	The **race car** has to obey an instruction
Preconditions	The race car is placed on a starting grid in a racing direction The race car is stopped The global trajectory is calculated ahead of the race The **green flag** is shown
Trigger	The race car pilot runs the single racing scenario
Name	Single_race_no_obstacles
Main success scenario	• The race car starts moving following the trajectory • The system calculates the local trajectory during the race • The race car follows the trajectory • The race car moves the designated number of laps • After the race car finishes the last lap it performs a **safe stop**
Success guarantee	The race car has finished the race The race car has crossed the starting line and stopped
Name	Single_race_no_obstacles

Extensions	1. The **red flag** received during the race
	     • The race car recalculates a global plan to perform an emergency stop
	     • The race car performs an emergency stop
	 2. The **yellow flag** is received during the race
	     • The system sets the speed limit according to the received value
	     • The race car finishes the race following the global trajectory and not exceeding the new speed limit
	 3. The difference between the calculated (desired) location and real (according to the sensors) location is more than a given threshold
	     • The race car recalculates a global plan to perform an emergency stop
	     • The race car performs an emergency stop

Stakeholders and interests	• **Race car pilot** (operates the race car) • Roborace management (sets the race goals and policies) • **Race Control Unit** (requests the race car to return to pit) • Roborace operations managers (set up and maintain the hardware)
	Note that the steps of the use case do not match the basic flow of the use case listed in section **G.5.1**. This is because section G.5 lists an overview of the key use cases, whereas detailed use cases in section S.4 distinguish use case triggers, preconditions, and main flow steps.

5.3 The Roborace

Table 5.7 Use Case 4. Race with virtual static obstacles

Name	Single_race_with_static_obstacles
Scope	System
Level	Business summary
Primary actor	**Race car pilot**
Context of use	The **race car** has to obey an instruction
Preconditions	The race car is placed on a starting grid in a racing direction The race car is stopped The global trajectory is calculated ahead of the race The **green flag** is shown
Trigger	The race car pilot runs the race with virtual static obstacles scenario
Name	Single_race_with_static_obstacles
Main success scenario	• The race car starts moving following the trajectory • The coordinates of the obstacles and bonuses are received from the Roborace in real time when moving • The system calculates the local trajectory to collect bonuses and avoid obstacles • The race car follows the trajectory • The race car moves the designated number of laps • After the race car finishes the last lap, it performs a **safe stop**
Success guarantee	The race car has finished the race, collecting the highest possible number of bonuses and avoiding all obstacles The race car has crossed the starting line and stopped
Extensions	A. It is not possible to avoid an obstacle B. To collect a bonus, the race car has to hit the obstacle
Stakeholders and interests	• **Race car pilot** • Roborace management (sets the race goals and policies) • **Race Control Unit** (requests the car to return to pit) • Roborace operations managers (set up and maintain the hardware)

S.6 Verification and Acceptance Criteria

 This section may contain verification and acceptance criteria at different levels of abstraction. It can be a high-level requirement to pass the homologation procedure, as stated in requirement S.6.1. It can be a collection of test cases that must be passed to demonstrate that the software meets the requirements. We discuss the relation of scenarios and test cases in Chap. 3.

S.6.1 The software must pass the homologation procedure conducted by the Roborace.

5.3.5 Project

P.1 Roles

 This section lists the personnel available for the project and the prospects of additional personnel recruitment.

Table 5.8 Project Participants

Position	Project role	Core competencies
Team Principal	Project Manager	
	Developer, Tester, Documenter	Car dynamics, system optimization, SLAM algorithms
Senior Robotics Software Engineer	Developer, Tester, Documenter	System optimization, cyber-physical systems, car dynamics
Senior Robotics Software Engineer	Developer, Tester, Documenter	Machine learning, racing algorithms

P.1.1 The project team includes the team principal, three software engineers who are 100% dedicated to the project, and four team members who dedicate 25–50% of their time to the project.

P.1.2 The core competencies of the full-time team members are shown in Table 5.8.

P.1.3 The software engineers responsible for the specific software modules perform requirements analysis, software development, and testing.

P.1.4 Due to the pandemic, the team members currently work remotely from different locations.

P.2 Imposed Technical Choices

 We aim to be as less restrictive as possible while describing imposed technical choices. It is up to the project team to take the decisions within the limitations listed below.

P.2.1 The software architecture and limitations are defined by the **Devbot's** hardware setup:

- P.2.1.1 **NVIDIA Drive PX2** is used for data and/or computational intense algorithms (perception and planning parts of the software).
- P.2.1.2 **Speedgoat Real-Time ECU** is used for highly time critical but less complex algorithms: sensor fusion, odometry information collection, and vehicle control.
- P.2.1.3 **Offline hardware** generates a map of a **racetrack** and creates an optimal **raceline** based on **lidar** and **GNSS** data collected.

P.3 Schedule, Milestones, and Deliverables

 Since project deliverables depend on the schedule and mission goals of the championship, we devote this section to the information related to the championship schedule and rules.

P.3.1 Project milestones correspond to the Roborace championship events. The schedule is a subject to change and will be updated in the course of a project.

P.3.2 The schedule for season Beta is shown in Table 5.9.

5.3 The Roborace

Table 5.9 Season Beta schedule

Date	Mission	Round	Key rules
Sept 24, 2020	Mission 1	Round 1	Each round is a six-lap race with a mixed reality **loots** and obstacles. Avoid virtual obstacles, hit virtual collectibles
Sept 25, 2020	Mission 1	Round 2	
Oct 29, 2020	Mission 1.1	Round 1	There are two types of objects for the event. Obstacles to avoid: every time an obstacle is struck, it adds to the result time 2 s. Collectables to hit: once an object of this type is collected, it subtracts 2 s from the result time
Oct 30, 2020	Mission 1.1	Round 2	
Dec 11, 2020	Mission 2	Round 3	Each round is a five-lap race with a mixed reality **loots** and obstacles. Teams get +5 s for any obstacle object that is struck. Teams get −1 s for any **loot** that is collected. Objects are to be revealed at least 200 m from the **car**

Date	Mission	Round	Key rules
Dec 12, 2020	Mission 2	Round 4	
Feb 13, 2021	Mission 3	Round 5	Each round is a five-lap race with a mixed-reality **loots** and obstacles. Teams get +30 s for any obstacle object that is struck. Teams get −2 s for any **loot** that is collected. Objects are to be revealed at least 200 m from the **car**
Feb 14, 2021	Mission 3	Round 6	
Apr 6, 2021	Mission 3.1	Round 7	Each round is a five-lap race with a mixed reality **loots** and obstacles. Teams have a 20-min session and two attempts in each round to finish the race. Teams get +30 s for any obstacle object that is struck. Teams get −2 s for any **loot** that is collected. Dynamic obstacles are moving at a fixed velocity between 10 and 100 kph. Objects are to be revealed at least 150 m from the **car**
Apr 7, 2021	Mission 3.1	Round 8	

Date	Mission	Round	Key rules
Apr 20, 2021	Mission 4	Round 9	Each round is a five-lap race with Mixed Reality **Gizmos**. Every time the **Devbot 2.0** hits the **Gizmo**, it receives a penalty or a reward to the result time. Each team has a 20-min session and two attempts in each round to finish the race. Penalties and Rewards: +30 s for any obstacle that is struck; −2 s for any **loot** that is collected; −20 s for every **ghost car** that is overtaken; +30 s for every **ghost car** hit; **Gizmos** reveal at least 150 m from the **Devbot 2.0**
Apr 21, 2021	Mission 4	Round 10	

P.4 Tasks and Deliverables

Although section P.4 must include the main project tasks according to the **Minimum Requirements Outcome principle**, we decided not to duplicate the project plan that has this information and to reference it instead.

P.4.1 Tasks and deliverables are listed in the project plan.

P.5 Required Technology Elements

In this section, we list the technology necessary for the successful completion of the project. Simulation facilities, mentioned in requirement P.5.1, combine software and hardware. The particular setup of a simulator is to be determined later in the project.

P.5.1 Since the access to **Devbot 2.0** practice sessions is very limited, the project success heavily depends on simulation facilities.

P.6 Risk and Mitigation Analysis

In this section, we list potential risks and their mitigation strategies.

P.6.1 **Unpredictability**.

- P.6.1.1 **Risk**: Producing autonomous race car software is partially a research task, since similar systems have not been developed before. Consequently, it is potentially possible that the team is not able to reach mission goals within the provided time frame.
- P.6.1.2 **Mitigation**: split the expected mission deliverable into chunks, so that if the mission goal is not reached completely, it is reached partially and a race car has a reasonable performance.

P.7 Requirements Process and Report

Requirements P.7.1 and P.7.2 describe the requirements process. We also use this section to accumulate the links to documentation gathered during requirements elicitation (P.7.3).

P.7.1 Project requirements are specified according to the PEGS approach. The current document serves as a compilation of all requirements-related information for the project. Whenever necessary, it contains links to requirements sources and requirements code elements.

P.7.2 Due to the limited size of a team and the competitive nature of the Roborace championship, the requirements evolve along with the championship's progress, and requirements prioritization changes as well.

5.4 Industrial and Other Use Cases

P.7.3   The links to the minutes of requirements elicitation events and outputs of other elicitation activities are collected below:

- P.7.3.1   First elicitation meeting
- P.7.3.2   Second elicitation meeting

5.4 Industrial and Other Use Cases

At the time of writing this companion book, we are aware of one industrial usage of the PEGS: the Streamlining Workforce Management.[3] This case study is discussed in the lessons learned (see Sect. 6.6).

Let us also mention the ATCO Eats case study, used in the Requirements Engineering class of **McMaster University**. The HTML version is freely available at https://ace-lectures.github.io/atco-eats/.

 The companion book use case (see Sect. 5.2) can also be considered as a real-life use case as it has been concretely used for this book writing.

---

[3] https://library.constructor.org/node/97

Lessons Learned 6

Prerequisite
This chapter shares our experience applying the PEGS approach. This **companion book** was written almost 2 years after the publication of **The Handbook** because we wanted to collect as much feedback as possible from projects, teaching, tutorials, presentations, and discussions with colleagues.

What You Will Find in This Chapter
The results of practicing the PEGS approach are compiled in this **companion book** (FAQ, templates, case studies), and this chapter provides our feedback on:

- Teaching at the university level (Toulouse, **Constructor University**, **McMaster University**)
- Writing the requirements for a real start-up
- Providing tutorials at the IEEE International Requirements Engineering Conference

What You Will Not Find in This Chapter
Even though the book was written over a period of 2 years, we still need long-term feedback to share, in the sense of having several reviews of requirements books, for example. Is the standard plan suitable for maintenance and evolution? How can concrete return on investment from applying PEGS be evaluated? What is the learning effort to adequately apply PEGS in industry? What is students' feedback on the practicality of PEGS in their post-graduate job? All these questions will have to wait for the next edition of this **companion book**.

6.1 Producing OO Requirements

The study is based on a controlled experiment conducted as a part of the "OO Analysis and Design" course delivered by **Sophie Ebersold** at the University of Toulouse, followed by a questionnaire. This course introduces **UML** as a requirements modeling language. In total, 31 students participated in the experiment: bachelor's students in their third year and master's students in their first year. **Sophie Ebersold** and **Mariya Naumcheva** provided students with a textual description of a case study, which they further used to elicit requirements and produce various requirements artifacts.

The experiment was split into two parts. In the first part (1.5 h), **Sophie Ebersold** presented the theory on OO requirements to students. The students were already familiar with **UML** and scenario modeling. Further, they were asked to describe two scenarios for each of the two given use cases according to a provided template. In the second part (4.5 h), students were randomly split into two groups (with two course instructors) and had to complete two tasks:

- (2–3 h) Students of Group 1 specified OO requirements for the first use case. Students of Group 2 produced a sequence diagram for the first use case.
- (2–3 h) Students of Group 1 worked on a sequence diagram for the second use case, and students of Group 2 specified OO requirements for the second use case.

After submitting the results of their work, the students filled out an online questionnaire. The questionnaire included two types of questions. Single-choice questions were formulated as statements that participants had to evaluate based on a Likert scale ("Strongly disagree," "Disagree," "Agree," "Strongly agree," "No opinion"). We used those questions to collect quantitative feedback on using OO requirements. We also used open questions to collect additional qualitative feedback, such as (1) the difficulties the participants faced applying the approach and (2) how the suggested approach helped students improve their **UML**-based specifications.

Among the respondents, 26% declared it was hard to understand and produce OO requirements, whereas 43% had a positive experience, and 30% were neutral. The experiment participants stated that they were not familiar enough with contracts, that not enough examples were provided, and that there was not enough practice.

The questionnaire responses indicate that OO requirements techniques helped students improve their **UML** specifications in the following ways:

- To think of elements we had not thought of, for example, additional preconditions
- To discover details that need to be added to features
- To better define and implement use cases
- To identify alternative scenarios for the system's use cases
- To better analyze the requirements globally for a specification

6.2 Concrete Use of a PEGS Book as an Initial Set of Requirements

Starting from the PEGS books of the Library Management System (the complete specification can be found in Sect. 5.1), two groups of six students from the University of Toulouse-Jean Jaurès (B.Sc. level) had 4 weeks to provide an implementation of the LMS. They noticed some inconsistencies or missing requirements in the specification, such as the frequency and duration of reminder emails, which were added later. They also noticed that the goals and system books stated that an ordinary user could create a customer account, but nowhere did they specify how a bookseller account was created. For security reasons, a user (e.g., a recruit) cannot create a bookseller account himself. Therefore, it has been decided and added to the specifications that only the bookshop manager, as Web site administrator, can create or assign an account to the bookshop manager, who will create accounts for his employees.

Over the course of 4 weeks, the students successfully developed a fully functional library management system. One site is here: https://limitless-harbor-51820-1d6827a32eb8.herokuapp.com/. Its source code is available at https://mi-git.univ-tlse2.fr/matthias.nadal/projet_bibliotheque.

This constitutes a proof of concept, showing that a PEGS specification enables developers to provide a system that verifies the requirements supplied in an ad hoc manner. As a client and supplier of the requirements, **Sophie Ebersold** interacted with the students. The clarifications mentioned above were the only subjects of interaction.

The project was developed completely autonomously.

6.3 Requirements Engineering Course in Toulouse (2024)

In 2024, **J.-M. Bruel** has taught the requirements engineering course of the University of Toulouse-Jean Jaurès' Master in Software Engineering on its MI0A112T module (Fig. 6.1).

The slides from this course are freely available at the **companion website**, as well as those related to **The Handbook** chapters.

The course was an introduction to requirements engineering (24 h), project-based, and fully dedicated to the PEGS approach (for the first year). A set of slides for each **The Handbook** chapter introduced during the course (Preface and chapters 1 to 3) were realized for this course. The additional set of slides was mainly used to connect with other courses or to present the project inputs and assignments.

Fig. 6.1 Slides excerpt

6.3.1 Active Learning

After gradually introducing the concepts, we have used the **Elaastic** platform to practice them, which we highly recommend the reader to explore. Elaastic is a Web platform that helps teachers and learners implement active learning. We asked the students to provide examples of requirements categories during face-to-face courses. The students had to answer the question by providing written argumentation and were asked about their confidence degree. Elaastic allowed them to confront their point of view by anonymously accessing the contributions of others, giving their opinion, and possibly changing their answer. The sequence ended with sharing the results, which created the opportunity to discuss their contributions and assessments.

6.3.2 Projects

For the project, the students (in groups of max three students) had to choose between three case studies:

- The Library Management Systems (for which we had a solution; see Sect. 5.1)
- The "Backup Power Supply," a classical realistic safety-critical system, used in a complementary course on formal requirements
- The "BAL 3000 Turbo Max Pro," a fake futuristic smart mailbox they had invented for a play as part of their communication course

Using **GitHub classroom**, the repositories of all the groups could be followed, and regular feedback to students were facilitated (see Fig. 6.2).

6.3 Requirements Engineering Course in Toulouse (2024)

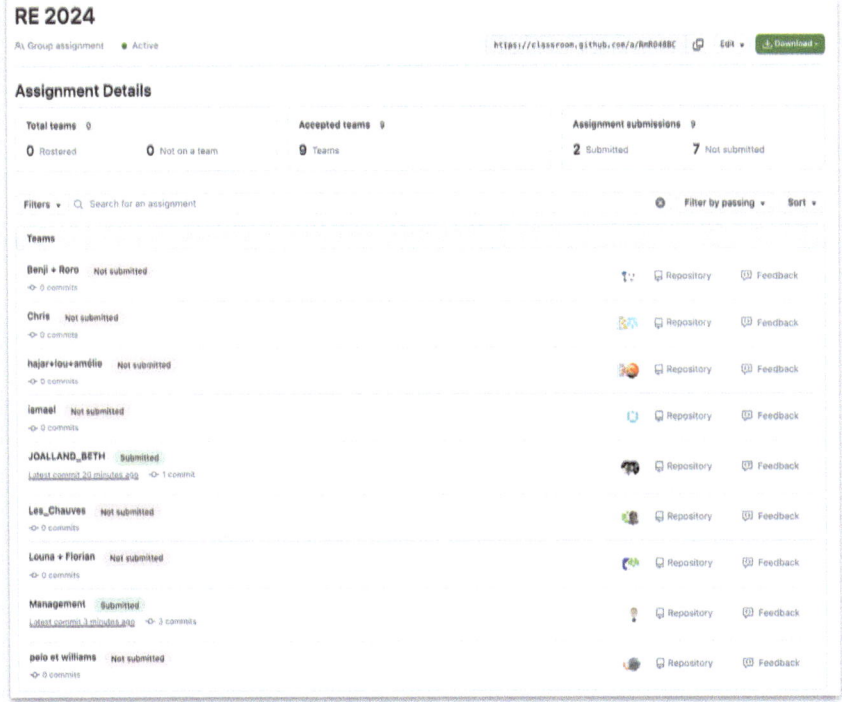

Fig. 6.2 Use of GitHub classroom

6.3.3 Outcomes

The main benefit of introducing the concepts was the course discussions about their pros and cons, ambiguities, or the usefulness of such or such categories. The cheatsheet (available at the **companion website**, see Fig. 6.3) was distributed to the students, and having a well-defined list of categories helped the students structure their thoughts and analysis.

A side (but very useful for teachers) benefit from imposing the standard plan (also noticed in the **McMaster University** experiment, see Sect. 6.5) is the grading of the project reports. In classical projects, when students are given the freedom to structure their requirements, the process of comparing and evaluating these reports can be quite time-consuming. A structured plan can significantly reduce this time.

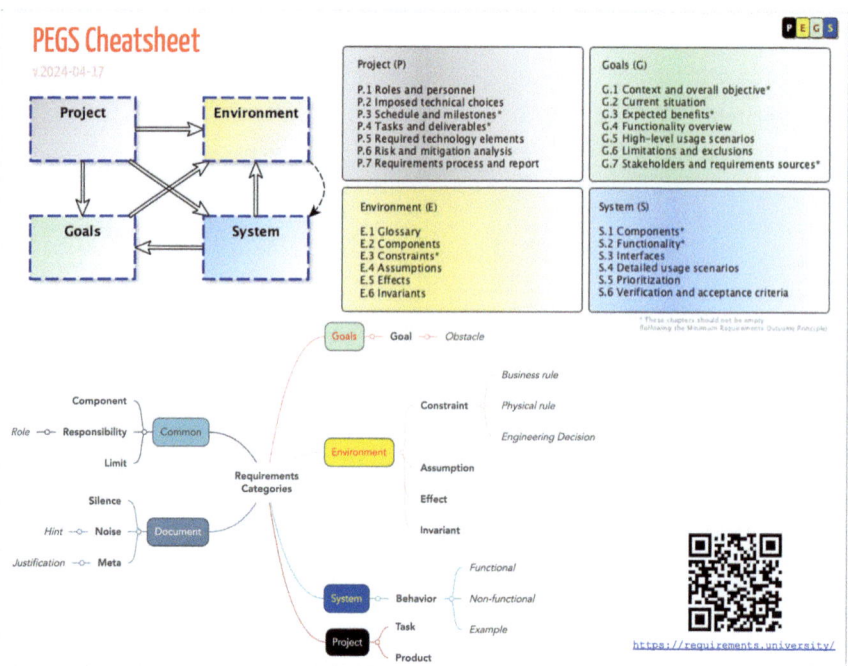

Fig. 6.3 Useful cheatsheet for PEGS course. https://requirements.university/

6.4 Producing PEGS Requirements: A Study at the Constructor University

As part of the "requirements engineering" course at the **Constructor University**, students produced a PEGS specification for the Library Management System (the LMS case study is presented in Sect. 5.1).

In this section, we report mistakes and confusion observed in the provided requirements documents:

- A statement "E.3.1. Library operation hours" in chapter **E.3—Constraints** is not a constraint because it does not express a Boolean property. An example of a constraint could be "E.3.1. Library operation hours are 9 am–9 pm." However, we must still evaluate whether it is a constraint and how it constrains a system or a project.
- Having terms that are not specified in a glossary.
- Missing definitions of "book" and "book instance" in the glossary. Suppose there is a potential ambiguity between the concepts, such as a book (as a separate edition) and a book instance (as a book copy, there can be several copies for one book). In that case, it must be covered in the glossary.
- An attempt to list all possible scenarios of interacting with the system, including alternatives and exceptions, in chapter **S.4—Detailed usage scenarios**. Even for

a relatively small system, such as LMS, it led to numerous scenarios, all listed but unspecified. Detailed usage scenarios must include postcondition or satisfaction criteria, at least for the most important scenarios.
- Confusing environment constraints with limitations and inclusions. Limitations and exclusions concern what the system will not address due to a project team's decision (what falls outside the project's scope). Constraints concern what the system will not do due to restrictions imposed by the environment, such as business rules. For example, "The system will not allow multiple patrons to check out one book at the same time" is a constraint since it specifies how the system's "check out" function will work. An example of a limitation is "The system will not handle payments" since it states that some functionality falls out of the project's scope.
- Providing risks and mitigation analysis for the system under development rather than for the project. Chapter **P.6—Risks and mitigation analysis** is devoted to potential obstacles to meeting the project schedule. Risk analysis of the product pertains to a business plan.

6.5 McMaster University (2024)

McMaster University has instantiated the PEGS framework on its COMPSCI/SFWRENG-3RA3 course (dedicated to requirements and security). Unlike the other feedback from this chapter, the specificity of this feedback is the large cohort involved (~230 students, mixed between software engineering, mechatronics, and computer science)! The course was taught by one instructor (**Sébastien Mosser**) and six teaching assistants over 12 weeks.

The course was mostly based on a term-long project where students worked in groups of three. For the project, all instructions were given on day 1. The input consisted of the minutes of a briefing with a client, which was associated with an "Ask me Anything Q&A" session (1 h, weekly, online). The expected outcome was the Software Requirements Specification (SRS) using the PEGS template and controlled by a PEGS-compatible Kanban (see Fig. 6.4).

The project is term-long to allow students to build up a proper understanding of complex requirements. However, as this is the first time in their curriculum where they are in control of requirements writing, mistakes are inevitable. Two optional "windows of opportunities" were introduced during the term to support students' learning. They simulate time slots during which customers' representatives can review partial SRS and provide feedback to the students. These windows are optional. The student can decide to wing it and deliver everything on the last day of the term. However, as requirements engineering is an incremental process, we encourage students to use it by providing opportunities for extra credit if they do so. They can claim such extra marks by adding an appendix at the end of their SRS explaining how the received feedback was used to improve the final delivery.

From a pure software engineering point of view, these "Windows of Opportunity" are agile sprints in disguise. This is a way to uniformize the students' background

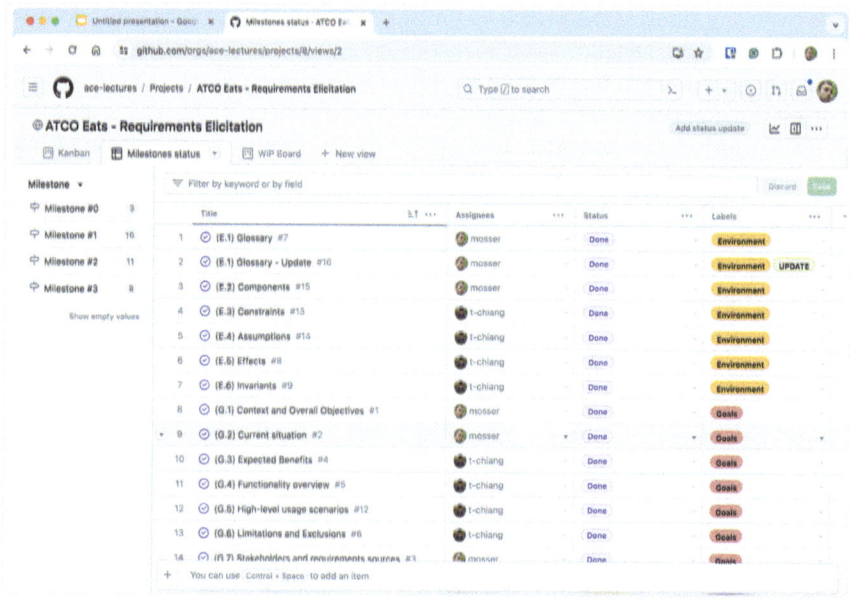

Fig. 6.4 Using project tracking (Kanban)

knowledge, as, for example, mechatronics and computer science students might not be familiar with agile development yet. At the project implementation level, they were defined using the GitHub milestone concept.

6.5.1 First Window of Opportunity

- Focus on:
  - Understanding customers' needs
  - Capturing high-level requirements

For the Goals book, the focus was to identify and analyze the context and the overall objective. The study of the current situation led to a single *Statement of Needs*. The stakeholders were modeled through Persona. For this first step, the expected benefits were mainly the goals' modeling, a functionality overview (only five functional requirements and two non-functional requirements were needed).

Only three chapters (**E1—Glossary**, **E.5—Effects**, and **E.6—Invariants**) were required for the Environment book. The objective was to help students focus on the requirements vocabulary and the impact (or absence of impact) of the system on the world.

For the project, students were asked to think about risks early so that they could "plan for the worst." They had to describe how they will interact with stakeholders as part of requirements elicitation. This step is partially influenced by the fact that

3RA3 as a security **component** is part of McMaster's curriculum and thinking about risk early is a way to introduce discussions about security later.

6.5.2 Second Window of Opportunity

- Focus on:
  - Reaching the system level

For the Goals book, the focus was on describing the high-level Usage Scenarios (use case diagrams, scenario modeling) and the limitations and exclusions to precisely define the scope of the product.

For the Environment book, the focus was on the remaining chapters (**E.3—Constraints, E.4—Assumptions**, and **E.2—Components**). For the components, the focus was on the external ones the system is interacting with. The vocabulary (**E1—Glossary**) was refined and formalized with a class diagram. The students were asked to make sure everything was consistent so that requirements could be refined at the system level and to make a difference between requirement analysis and design.

For the System book, **components** were listed, and a **UML** component diagram was added (**S.1—Components**). In addition, **S.3—Interfaces, S.2—Functionality**, and **S.6—Verification and Acceptance Criteria** were detailed. The students were asked to work on traceability between sections and pushed for consistency checking.

 Components are usually design artifacts. We use them to bridge this course with other design courses at McMaster, showing how "high-level" **components** used here only to organize the requirements can be later on reused/refined in their "Software Design-Large Scale Architecture" course and then capstone project.

6.5.3 Final Delivery

- Focus on:
  - Finalizing the SRS
  - Ensuring consistency between requirements

For the System book, **S.5—Prioritization** was added (using **MoSCoW**), and **S.6—Verification and Acceptance Criteria** was enforced. Students were asked to prioritize requirements to justify how they would perform such prioritization. The justification process was more important than the outcome.

For the Project book, the main chapters were filled out (**P.1—Role and Personnel, P.2—Imposed Technical Choices, P.5—Required Technology Elements, P.3—Schedule and Milestones, P.4—Tasks and Deliverables**, and **P.6—Risk and Mitigation Analysis**).

6.5.4 Measurements

As McMaster Software Engineering and Mechatronics Engineering programs are accredited in Canada, each instructor needs to measure the so-called Graduate Attribute to report on the learning outcome of each cohort and participate in a feedback report at the program level. Students' outcomes are classified as "below expectations" (BE), "marginal" (MA), "meeting expectations" (ME), or "exceeding expectations" (XE).

> In Fig. 6.5:
> - Red is "below expectation" (failing a given dimension of the course)
> - Orange is "marginal"
> - Green is Ok (meet expectation)
> - Purple is amazing (exceed expectations)

For 3RA3, 12 attributes need to be measured. While one should take this observation with a grain of salt (new instructor, only one cohort observed, using a generic accreditation framework, and not a controlled experiment), we observe a clear imbalance in the following measurements:

- Domain understanding:
  - 1.4: *Understanding requirement process; domain understanding, requirements elicitation, evaluation, and documentation.*
  - 2.1: *Specify and analyze scenarios using diagrammatic notations and formal methods; analyze and specify security properties of simple computing systems.*
- Correctness of requirements:
  - 5.1: *Specify and analyze scenarios using diagrammatic notations and formal methods.*
  - 7.1: *Requirements specification and documentation; correct problematic requirements.*

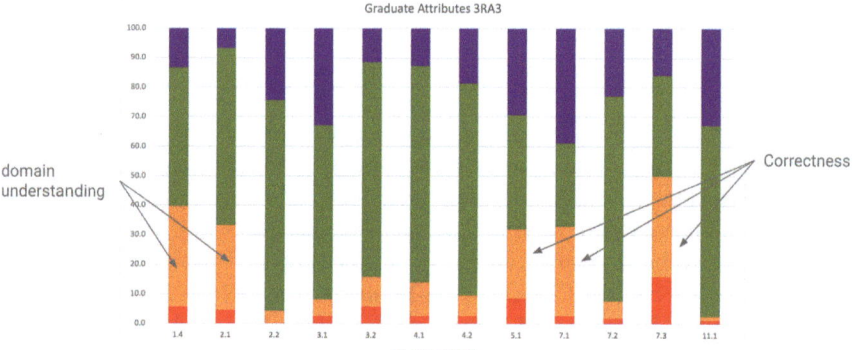

Fig. 6.5 Graduate attributes

– 7.3: *Requirements specification and documentation; provide rigorous requirements.*

Overall, the PEGS framework helped the cohort meet expectations on everything but the two hardest points: understanding the domain and building correct requirements. Where previous cohorts were confused by the organization of requirements, using the template cleared out all of these concerns. It is a significant improvement that only "understanding the domain" and "requirements correctness" are opportunities for improvement, as these two dimensions require time, practice, and experience, which students will acquire in their upcoming industrial internships or projects.

6.6 PEGS Requirements for the MVP (2023)

An application of the PEGS approach for producing requirements for the MVP product in a start-up project is reported by a master's student of **Constructor Institute of Technology**. Evaluating her experience of applying the approach, she comes to the following conclusions:

- The PEGS approach provides a holistic perspective on the developed system. The Goals, Environment, and Project books are written so that anyone can grasp the details of the system, whereas the Systems book has more technical writing. The Goals book and the Project book seem to represent parts of a business plan for a start-up, yet it does not substitute for it.
- Numbering of every paragraph, in the Environment and System books, may interrupt the reader's flow in the Goals and Project books. Some sections, such as "What the system should not do" and "Imposed technical choices," substantially affected the project's incubation and brought up ideas that could have been missed otherwise.
- It might be beneficial to provide a manual on how to read the PEGS specification (which part is meant for which party) for its future readers.

Evaluating this work, we may note the confusion that comes from the "PEGS" abbreviation: for the sake of connotation, the order of letters in the name of the approach does not correspond to the order of the books: although there is no strict order in completing the books, the requirements elicitation starts with goals, followed by **environment** analysis. The requirements specification, produced linearly, starts with the Goals book and is followed by the Environment, System, and Project books.

6.7 RE Conference Tutorials (2023 and 2024)

The **IEEE International Requirements Engineering Conference**[1] is issuing a call for tutorials every year.

With **The Handbook** published at the end of 2022, the authors, who worked closely on its content, submitted a tutorial for RE'23. It was accepted and given by **J.-M. Bruel** in Hannover.[2] After this successful tutorial, **Sébastien Mosser** and **J.-M. Bruel** submitted another one for RE'24, which was dedicated this time to teaching requirements engineering. It was also accepted and given by **J.-M. Bruel** at Reykjavik.[3] These tutorials, which were highly practical and immediately applicable, provided the attendees with concrete guidance, beneficial for both practitioners and teachers. Despite the diverse numbers (5 in 2023 and 16 in 2024) and background (students, practitioners, teachers, quality assessors, etc.) of the attendees, the benefit of those tutorials, apart from spreading the word about PEGS, was to see and discuss the initial reactions. A standard plan and a list of precise categories were initially considered constraining frames. However, discussing the advantages and showing the adaptation possibilities of the approach waived the initial apprehensions.

---

[1] The most renowned international conference on the topic.
[2] See https://conf.researchr.org/track/RE-2023/RE-2023-tutorials.
[3] See https://conf.researchr.org/track/RE-2024/RE-2024-tutorials.

Appendix A: Glossary

There are two ways to write a glossary. In a learning approach, we would have used a topologically sorted list of terms, defining complex terms from the previously defined, simple ones. This is the approach taken in **The Handbook** (which does not have a Glossary section as such), where terms are defined "on the fly" while they are introduced. In this **companion book**, we have a referencing approach for this section and used an alphabetically sorted list. This section is a reference entry for terms used in the book and **The Handbook**.

The page numbers in this glossary do not refer to this particular book but to **The Handbook** (the 2022 edition).

We follow in this glossary the **Acronym Principle**:

In glossary entries introducing acronyms, do not just expand: explain.

An additional list of entries (particularly useful if you prepare for a certification) can be found at IREB.[1]

Abstractness	A **system** requirement is abstract if it specifies a desired **system property** without prescribing or favoring specific design or implementation choices.
Actor	An element (a system **component** or a human) in charge in a **responsibility**.
Ambiguity	See **non-ambiguity**.

---

[1] https://www.ireb.org/en/cpre/cpre-glossary/

© The Editor(s) (if applicable) and The Author(s), under exclusive license to Springer Nature Switzerland AG 2025
J.-M. Bruel et al., *Applying Requirements and Business Analysis*, https://doi.org/10.1007/978-3-031-92160-5

API	Application Programming Interface, a set of functions and procedures allowing the creation of applications that access the features or data of an operating system, application, or other service.
Assumption	An **assumption**, also known as a precondition, is a **property** that we expect the **environment** to fulfill; the construction of the **system** takes it for granted. It is one of the requirement kinds defined in Sect. 2.1.3. See also **this section**.
Author	Person who produced a particular **requirement**.
Behavior	A behavior is the specification that the **system** must produce a certain outcome or behave in a certain way. It is one of the requirement kinds defined in Sect. 2.1.3.
BON	Business Object Notation, a method and graphical notation for high-level object-oriented analysis and design, extending the higher-level concepts of the Eiffel programming language.
CESAM	CESAMES Systems Architecting Method is a systems architecting and modeling framework that has achieved significant usage in industry, particularly in France.
Class	In object-oriented approaches to system modeling and structuring, a class is a system unit specifying a type of object with the associated operations and their properties.
Cluster	A coherent set of classes (components) whose development should be considered synchronously (see Sect. 2.3).
Completeness	A set of **requirements** is complete, or not, along six criteria: document, goal, scenario, environment, interface, and command-query completeness.
Component	A component requirement specifies that the **project**, **environment**, **goals**, or **system** shall contain a certain part. It is one of the requirement kinds defined in Sect. 2.1.3.
Consistency	A set of **requirements** is consistent if it contains no contradiction.
Constraint	A constraint is a **property** of the **environment** that restricts what the **system** and **project** can do. It is one of the requirement kinds defined in Sect. 2.1.3.
Correctness	An **environment** or **system** requirement is correct if it is compatible with actual project parameters, **properties** of the **environment** (**constraints**, **assumptions**, **effects**, **invariants**), organizational **goals**, and **stakeholder** expectations.
Delimitedness	A set of **goals** or **system** requirements is delimited if it specifies the scope of the future **system**, making it possible to determine what functionality lies beyond that scope.

Appendix A: Glossary

Effect	An effect, also known as a postcondition, is the specification of a change that an operation of the system may bring to the **environment**. It is one of the requirement kinds defined in Sect. 2.1.3.
Endorsement	A **requirement** is endorsed if it has been approved by all the **relevant** decision-makers.
Environment	An environment is the set of entities external to the **project** and **system** but with the potential to affect the **goals**, **project**, or **system** or to be affected by them.
Feasibility	A **system** (resp. **project**) requirement is feasible if it is possible, within the **constraints** of the **environment** and **goals**, to produce an implementation (resp. schedule) that satisfies it.
GDPR	General Data Protection Regulation, a set of regulation rules relating to the protection of natural persons with regard to the processing of personal data and rules relating to the free movement of personal data.
Goal	A goal is a result desired by an organization. A goal is a **need** of the target organization, which the **system** must address. See Sect. B.1.3 for the difference with **needs**.
GORE	Goal-Oriented Requirements Engineering, a branch of Requirements Engineering focusing on goals and their management.
IDE	Integrated Development Environment. The dedicated tool supporting the software development.
Invariant	An invariant is an **environment property** that the **system** must maintain. It is one of the requirement kinds defined in Sect. 2.1.3.
IREB	The International Requirements Engineering Board—a non-profit organization—is the provider of the most known certification in Requirements Engineering and a good source of useful materials.
Justifiability	A **project** or **system** requirement is justified if it helps reach a **goal** or satisfy a **constraint**.
Justification	A case of **meta-requirement**, also called a rationale, is an argument explaining the reason for a **property** of the **system** or **project** in terms of a **goal** or of an **environment** property. See Sect. 2.1.3.6.
Limit	Exclusion from scope of requirements. It is one of the requirement kinds defined in Sect. 2.1.3. See also section "Requirements Applying to All Dimensions".
LMS	Library Management System, one of the case study of this book.

Meta (Meta-requirement)	Property of requirements themselves. It is one of the requirement kinds defined in Sect. 2.1.3. See also section "Document Description".
Modifiability	A set of **requirements** is modifiable if it can be adapted in case of changes to **project**, **environment**, **goals**, or **system** properties, through an effort commensurate with the extent of the changes.
MoSCoW	An acronym to represent a priority scale, often used in Agile methods, to classify features or requirements. The scale, by order of priority, is as follows: **M**ust, **S**hould, **C**ould, and **W**ill (or Will not, in some cases).
Need	Needs are the underlying reasons for the existence of the **system**. See Sect. B.1.3 for the difference with **goals**.
Noise	Property that is in requirements but should not. It is one of the requirement kinds defined in Sect. 2.1.3.
Non-ambiguity	A set of **requirements** is unambiguous if none of its elements is so expressed as to lend itself to two significantly different understandings.
Non-functional	(To be continued). It is one of the three requirement sub-kinds of **behavior**, defined in Sect. 2.1.3.
Obstacle	An obstacle is a **goal** consisting of removing or otherwise addressing a **property** of the current situation that has negative consequences for the target organization.
PEGS	Project, Environment, Goal, System, the four books structuring the standard requirements documentation. See Fig. 2.23 for more details on the dependability links between the four books.
Prioritization	A set of **system** requirements is prioritized if it includes for each of them a specification of its importance relative to the others, making it possible to make informed decisions if events in the course of the **project** make it necessary to renounce some functionality.
Product	A product requirement is the specification of an artifact as either produced by the **project** or needed by the **project**. It is one of the requirement kinds defined in Sect. 2.1.3.
Project	A project is the set of human processes involved in the planning, construction, operation, and revision of a **system**.
Property	A "property" as used in requirements is a Boolean trait of a **project, environment**, or **system**.
Rationale	See **justification**.
Readability	A **requirement** is readable if it can be readily understood by its intended audience.

Appendix A: Glossary

Relevant property, relevant statement	A **goal property** is relevant. A **property** of the **project** or **system** is relevant if it can affect or be affected by a **stakeholder**. A **property** of the **environment** is relevant if it can affect or be affected by the **project** or **system**. A **statement** of a **property** is relevant if the **property** is relevant.
Requirement	A requirement is a **relevant statement** about a **project**, **environment**, **goals**, or **system**.
Responsibility	A responsibility requirement specifies a certain **actor** is in charge of carrying out a certain **task** (for a **project** requirement) or **behavior** (for a **system** requirement). It is one of the requirement kinds defined in Sect. 2.1.3.
Role	A special case of **responsibility**: a human or an organizational responsibility.
RUP	Rational Unified Process, a comprehensive framework for project organization, introduced in the early 2000s, and strongly related to Unified Modeling Language, the de facto modeling notation.
Silence	Property that is not in requirements but should. It is one of the requirement kinds defined in Sect. 2.1.3.
SOI	System of Interest, the system under consideration or development.
Stakeholders	The stakeholders of a **project** are the groups of people recognized by the **project** as having the potential to affect, or be affected by, the **project**, **environment**, **goals**, or **system**.
Statement	A statement is a human-readable expression of a **property**.
System	A system is a set of related artifacts, devised to help meet certain **goals**.
Task	A task requirement is an activity that is a **component** of the **project**. It is one of the requirement kinds defined in Sect. 2.1.3.
TBD	To Be Determined: a part of the document that needs additional information. We recommend highlighting those parts and adding crucial complementary information (such as who, when, etc.). See the Document completeness rule in **Appendix D**.
Traceability	A **goals**, **system**, **project**, or **environment** requirement is traceable if it is possible to follow its consequences, both ways, in other project artifacts including design, implementation, and verification elements.
UML	Unified Modeling Language, the de facto standard for modeling.

URL Uniform Resource Locator, a (unique) reference to a Web source.

Verifiability A **system** (resp. **project**) requirement is verifiable if it is expressed in such a way as to allow determining whether a proposed implementation (resp. the sequence of events in the actual **project**) satisfies it.

Appendix B: Frequently Asked Questions

We have collected in that appendix a set of questions that were often asked during the early presentations of PEGS. They are not provided in a particular order but have been grouped by main concerns.

B.1. Kinds of Requirements and Specific Concepts

B.1.1. Business Analysis vs. Mission Analysis

What are the differences between *business analysis*, as used in **The Handbook**, and *mission analysis*, as defined in systems engineering approaches?

Business analysis can be summarized as identifying and defining business **needs** and finding solutions to business problems. In the context of systems engineering, it is sometimes called *mission analysis*.

Mission analysis is the process of identifying and analyzing the factors that can affect the successful completion of a mission. It involves assessing an organization's or individual's resources, capabilities, limitations, and external factors that may impact the mission. It is then narrower in scope, in the variety of the stakeholders, in the time frame, and in the outputs:

Scope
  Business analysis focuses on understanding and improving the operations of a business or organization. In contrast, mission analysis focuses on understanding and improving the likelihood of success for a specific mission or task.

Stakeholders
  Business analysis often involves working with many stakeholders, including business leaders, employees, customers, and shareholders. In contrast, mission analysis typically involves a smaller group of stakeholders, such as military or government personnel.

Time frame
  Business analysis is typically a long-term process involving ongoing analysis and improvement, while mission analysis often focuses on a specific, short-term goal or objective.

Output
  Business analysis often results in developing business requirements, business cases, and other documents that outline the proposed solutions to business problems. In contrast, mission analysis may result in developing plans, strategies, and tactics to achieve the mission.

B.1.2. Multiple Categories

Can a requirement belong to multiple categories (e.g., being both a limit and an invariant)?

No. If you hesitate between two or more, choose the one that makes the most sense.

B.1.3. Goals vs. Needs
What are the differences between a **goal** and a **need**?

 In requirements engineering, **goals** and **needs** are related but distinct concepts:

Goals
are high-level objectives that a system or product is intended to achieve. They are usually expressed in terms of what the system will do or enable the user to do. Goals are typically abstract and may be difficult to quantify or measure.

Needs
on the other hand are the underlying reasons for the existence of a system or product. They represent the deficiencies or problems the system or product intends to address. Needs are more concrete and specific than goals and are usually expressed in terms of what the system must do to meet the user's needs.

For example, consider a system being developed to help people manage their finances. A goal of this system might be to "help people make informed decisions about their financial future." The system might be designed to "provide accurate and up-to-date information about the user's spending and saving habits."

B.1.4. Actors

How are **actors** identified in PEGS?

 An actor is responsible of a task or a behavior and can be represented:
- As a `system component` (e.g., an input-output system monitoring some temperature value). It will be listed in the **S.1—Components** chapter.
- As a `human actor`, we will then use the term **role** to refer to its **responsibility** in PEGS. It will be listed in the **P.1—Roles and personnel** chapter.
- As an `environment component` (e.g., a data center). It will be listed in the **E.2—Components** chapter (Fig. B.1).

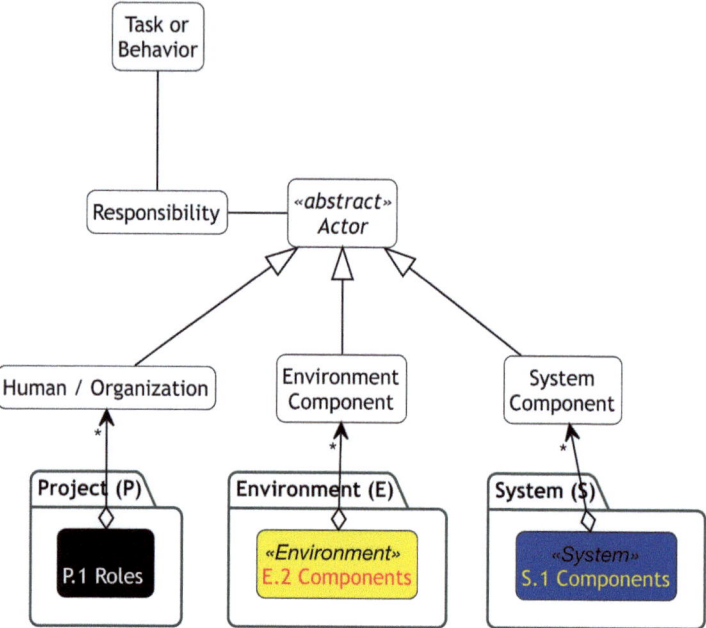

Fig. B.1 Different kinds of actors

Appendix B: Frequently Asked Questions

B.1.5. Constraints Versus Imposed Technical Choices

How to distinguish between **constraints** and imposed technical choices?

 An imposed technical choice is indeed a constraint. Nevertheless, it is better to separate them from the other **environment** constraints in a separate chapter. We advise to systematically check constraints and find any technical choice to move them to (or make sure they are referenced in) the corresponding chapter (**P.2— Imposed technical choices**).

B.1.6. Constraints Versus Assumptions

How to distinguish between **constraints** and **assumption**?

 The difference between a **constraint** and an **assumption** can sometimes seem fuzzy. It comes from the fact that the same condition can be a constraint for a certain domain (e.g., a network provider) and an **assumption** for another (e.g., a system developer using that network).
If an **environment** condition:
- **Restricts** what the implementation of the system can do: it is a constraint.
- **Facilitates** the implementation of the system: it is an **assumption**.

An equivalent characterization defines how the condition affects the work of the developers (defined as any people involved in the development of the system):
- A **constraint** makes the developers' work **harder** (by limiting the extent of what the system is permitted to do).
- An **assumption** makes the developers' work **easier** (by freeing the system from having to consider some cases).

The **following table** is a non-exhaustive list of characteristics that can help differentiate the two concepts (Table B.1).

B.1.7. Constraints Versus Obligations

The book does not talk about Obligations. How are they considered in the approach?

 Obligations are imposed constraints. As such, they belong to the kind **constraint**.

Table B.1 Assumption vs. Constraints

Assumptions	Constraints
Generally accepted as true without proof	Condition/restriction that limits the options/possibilities available
Typically *made about* the environment, project, etc.	Typically *imposed by* external factors
Usually made by the project team	Typically imposed from outside the team
Often made based on incomplete/uncertain information	Typically well-defined and clearly understood
May need to be validated	Are often justified or documented

B.1.8. Glossary Entries

How would you categorize glossary terms in the taxonomy of requirements?

 Referring to the table of categories on page 7 of **The Handbook**, section 1.4, the best match is **component**—specifically **component** of the environment.

B.1.9. Effect Versus Functional Requirement

How to distinguish between an effect and a functional requirement?

- If it describes a **change of property** induced by the development of the whole system, it is an effect.
- If the change described is brought by an **individual execution** (of software system or code), it is a functional requirement.

Let's imagine a campus where classrooms are equipped with some LED display (outside of each classroom) about the scheduled courses. An example effect of the system is "the display for every classroom shall indicate the occupation schedule for the room for the current 24-h period." An example functional requirement (addressing that effect) is, in the specification of a scheduling operation, "update the displays for all classrooms affected by the new scheduling."

+ TIP: Each effect requirement should be associated with at least one functional requirement.

B.1.10. Effect Versus Expected Benefits

How to distinguish between an effect and an expected benefit?

 See discussions on requirements 7 in **Appendix F**, 3-E.1.

B.1.11. Rationale

How are **rationales** managed in PEGS?

 We use the term **justification**. In PEGS, a **justification** is a case of **meta-requirement** that corresponds to an argument explaining the reason for a **property** of the System or Project in terms of a Goal or of an Environment property.

B.1.12. Interviews and Reviews

How are interviews reports and reviews managed in PEGS?

 Interviews and reviews play a critical role in requirements engineering, serving as essential techniques for gathering, validating, and refining requirements (see chapter 6 of **The Handbook** about gathering requirements). Whatever approach is used to conduct these crucial steps for requirements engineering, it is a valuable addition to the documentation.

We consider that the best place to describe the interviews and reviews processes is chapter **P.7—Requirements process and report**.

B.1.13. Software Architecture
Where should I describe my software architecture in PEGS?

While not fully in the scope of requirements engineering, integrating software architecture considerations can help create a strong foundation for the development of a software system that meets both the functional and non-functional needs of stakeholders. In addition, if the system of interest either already exists or is based on an existing one, this should be described in the requirements documentation.
Here are some examples of additional details that can be added:
- A **UML** component diagram in chapter **S.1—Components** or **E.2—Components** (whether they are internal or external)
- A domain model in chapter **E.1—Glossary**
- High-level APIs or a **UML** communication diagrams in chapter **S.3—Interfaces**
- A **UML** activity diagram could detail some of the use case in chapter **S.4—Detailed Usage Scenarios**

B.1.14. Security
How do I deal with specific (or crosscutting) concerns such as Security in PEGS?

Handling specific concerns, such as security, in requirements engineering is a common practice. For security aspects, the purpose is to ensure that the software system is designed, developed, and deployed with the necessary security measures to protect against potential threats and vulnerabilities.

Most of the requirements dedicated to a particular concern (such as security) will be expressed as constraints on either the system itself (chapter **E.3—Constraints**) or on the development (chapter **P.7—Requirement process and report**). We advise to also use chapter **S.5—Prioritization** to emphasize on the different aspects of the system's specific concerns. If a particular approach is dedicated to this concern or if specific artifacts need to be produced or if specific steps need to be validated in the process, these should be described in the **P.4—Tasks and deliverables** chapter.

B.2. Agile Approach

If I want to use PEGS, but I have already an Agile process to follow, where can I define my agile key artifacts?

Requirements engineering plays a crucial role in Agile approaches such as Scrum, although its implementation and emphasis may differ from traditional waterfall methodologies. In the following, we discuss some of the key concerns of Scrum and how PEGS can handle them.

Product Backlog

In Scrum, the product requirements are captured in the Product Backlog. The Product Backlog is a dynamic and prioritized list of user stories, features, enhancements, and bug fixes that need to be implemented over time. These items represent the requirements of the product. User stories are discussed in the next point due to their importance. We consider that features, enhancements, and bug fixes are development artifacts.

As such, classical product backlog artifacts do not need to be explicitly mentioned in one of the four books. Nevertheless:

- A list of features would make sense in chapter **S.2—Functionality**.
- Each artifact should **refer to at least one requirement**.

User Stories

Instead of detailed and exhaustive documentation of requirements, Agile methodologies use user stories (see chapter 7.2 of **The Handbook**). They are concise, informal descriptions of a feature from the perspective of the end-user or customer. These stories, while not being requirements as such, are an efficient way to illustrate them.

We consider that the best place to list them is the chapter **S.4—Detailed Usage Scenarios** where they might replace (or complement) `use cases`, for example, `Epic`, could be listed in **G.5—High-Level Usage Scenarios**.

Personas

A persona is a fictional representation of a particular user type or archetype that represents the various segments of the target audience. Personas encapsulate user characteristics, goals, needs, behaviors, and pain points.

As such, they can be detailed in a dedicated part of chapter **G.7—Stakeholders and Requirements Sources**.

Prioritization and Refinement

In agile methods, requirements are continuously prioritized based on their value and potential impact. The `Product Owner` (who should be listed in **P.1—Roles and Personnel**) is responsible for maintaining and prioritizing the Product Backlog.

We advise maintaining a **separate document** (which might be an appendix of the requirements documentation) that prioritizes the requirements (or user stories) with their reference to the requirements documentation. This allows to preserve the reference of the requirements while considering the required agility in treating them.

If not in a separate document, the chapter **S.5—Prioritization** can be used for this purpose, with a particular care of its versioning and dynamic nature if used in an agile context.

Sprint Planning

In Scrum, work is organized into time-bound iterations called sprints. During Sprint Planning, the team selects a set of user stories from the Product Backlog to work on in the upcoming sprint. The selected user stories are broken down into smaller tasks, helping the team better understand the requirements and estimate the work involved.

We consider that the best place to describe those planning is the chapter **P.3—Schedule and Milestones** (with complementary details potentially in **P.4—Tasks and Deliverables**).

B.3. Goal-Oriented Requirements Engineering

Goal-oriented approaches like KAOS (Knowledge Acquisition in Automated Specification) focus on capturing and analyzing goals and their relationships to derive system requirements. It helps ensure that the resulting system meets the intended goals and objectives of its stakeholders. Here's how PEGS fits into these approaches.

B.3.1. Goal Modeling and Decomposition
Can I use Goal-Oriented Requirements Engineering (GORE) with PEGS?

In KAOS, the primary focus is on modeling goals. These goals represent the desired outcomes that stakeholders want to achieve with the system. Goals are organized hierarchically, where higher-level goals are refined into more specific sub-goals. We consider that the best place to describe this hierarchy is the chapter **G.3—Expected Benefits**. The systematic referencing mechanisms should also enforce the traceability between sub-goals and goals.

B.3.2. Responsibility Modeling
How can I represent GORE responsibilities in PEGS?

KAOS introduces the concept of `agents` and `responsibilities`. Agents are entities that can contribute to achieving goals, and responsibilities define the actions or behaviors that agents must perform to satisfy specific goals.
Agents can be listed in:
- Chapter **G.7—Stakeholders and Requirements Sources**, if they are human
- Chapter **E.2—Components** if they are parts of the environment
- Chapter **S.1—Components** if they are specific parts of the system

Responsibilities can be specifically identified as such in Chapter **S.4—Detailed Usage Scenarios**.

Appendix C: Categories of Stakeholder

The following list does not aim to be exhaustive or prescriptive but to serve as a checklist to help avoid missing some important ones. Section 1.10.1 of **The Handbook** already provides a list, divided into the "target" groups (users or customers) and the "production" groups (involved in the development) of people. The following improved list is comprehensive and can be printed as a checklist.

C.1. Target Groups

> The following groups are stakeholders on the customer side.

- [ ] Primary Users of the future system (end users who directly interact with the product or system)
- [ ] Secondary Users of the future system (users who may not directly interact with the product but are affected by its use or outcomes)
- [ ] Potential Users (test groups when no real users are available)
- [ ] Users of the existing system (that will be replaced)
- [ ] Client Programmers (when the system will provide an **API**)
- [ ] Subject-Matter Experts (experts of the domain area covered by the system)
- [ ] Marketing and Sales (teams responsible for promoting and selling the product)
- [ ] Legal and Compliance Teams (ensuring the project complies with legal requirements and contracts)
- [ ] Regulators/Compliance Authorities (organizations or government bodies responsible for industry regulations)
- [ ] Customers (individuals or organizations that purchase or finance the product or service)
- [ ] Customers' customers (when the target system if for a client's customers usage)

- ☐ Labor unions (if the system will affect people's work conditions)
- ☐ Product Managers (those responsible for defining the product vision, strategy, and roadmap)
- ☐ Decision-makers (on target side)
- ☐ Executives/Leadership (senior management and executives with strategic interests)
- ☐ Sponsors (entities or individuals providing funding or resources for the project)
- ☐ Business Analysts (professionals who analyze business needs and translate them into requirements)
- ☐ Operations/IT Support (teams responsible for maintaining and supporting the product in the long term)
- ☐ Competitors (rival companies or products in the market)
- ☐ Suppliers/Vendors (those providing essential **component** or services for the project)
- ☐ Community and Public Interest Groups (organizations or individuals representing community interests)
- ☐ Financial Analysts/Investors (individuals or entities with a financial stake in the project's success)
- ☐ Environmental/Sustainability Groups (organizations concerned with ecological and sustainability aspects)
- ☐ Ethical and Social Responsibility Advocates (stakeholders who focus on ethical and social aspects of the project)
- ☐ Internal Users/Employees (persons who may use the system for internal processes)
- ☐ Support and Helpdesk (teams responsible for addressing user inquiries and issues)
- ☐ Security Experts (professionals responsible for ensuring the security of the product)
- ☐ Human Resources (who may have requirements related to employee roles and responsibilities)
- ☐ Government/Regulatory Bodies (agencies overseeing industry-specific regulations)
- ☐ Non-governmental Organizations (external organizations with a vested interest in the project's impact)
- ☐ Academic Institutions (researchers or educators with an interest in the project's outcomes)
- ☐ Media and Press (entities that may cover or report on the project)
- ☐ Alliances and Partners (organizations collaborating on the project)

Appendix C: Categories of Stakeholder 143

C.2. Production Groups

> The following groups are stakeholders on the development side.

- ☐ Project Managers (the persons directing the development)
- ☐ Testers/Quality Assurance (individuals responsible for testing the product to ensure it meets requirements)
- ☐ Testers (to ascertain conformance of any future implementation to the requirements)
- ☐ Documenters (to ease the production of user manuals for example)
- ☐ Trainers (if the future system requires training)
- ☐ Designers/UX Experts (those responsible for the user interface and overall user experience)
- ☐ HCI Experts (or ergonomics experts, for Human-Computer Interfaces)
- ☐ Developers/Engineering Team (the technical team responsible for building and implementing the solution, to avoid "pie-in-the-sky" systems requirements)
- ☐ Open-source Community (for open-source projects)
- ☐ **GDPR** Experts (to assess conformance with the regulation)
- ☐ Legal Experts (for any Intellectual property or licensing issues)
- ☐ Ethical Experts (for concerns such as gender balance)
- ☐ Health and Safety Experts (for hazard control)

 This list has been improved by using **ChatGPT** v.3.5!

Appendix D: Principles and Good Practice Rules

The Handbook includes a certain number of explicit, and sometimes implicit, *rules*: good practices or elements to measure the quality of the requirements. We list the 36 we have collected in the following section.

Requirements
(See 2.1.1 of **The Handbook***.)*

> Any successful project must involve a requirements effort.

Well, if you're reading this book, you must be already aware of this principle. We advise that you nevertheless check if you have considered a systematic review on updating them regularly (following the **Requirements Elaboration Principle**).

Requirements Questions
(See 2.1.2 of **The Handbook***.)*

> Take advantage of the requirements process to ensure that important questions about the Project, Environment, Goals, and System are raised and addressed at the proper time.

Requirements Nature
(See 2.1.3 of **The Handbook***.)*

> Requirements are software.

We know this sounds weird at first! But give it a try. What are the characteristics of a code? We can cite: to be executed by a computing device, written by people, expressed in a notation, can be combined with other elements, subject to change, interacts with other elements, subject to systematic recording of its content, properties, and evolution in a database of software elements, a process known as configuration management. Well, apart from the first one, all the others apply to requirements and to other software artifacts such as test plans, design specifications or diagrams, etc. We advocate that considering requirements also as software artifacts allows to possess the same benefits.

Requirements Evolution
(See 2.1.4 of **The Handbook**.*)*

> Requirements are a living asset of any project, subject to evolution. They must be adapted and kept up to date throughout the project.

Requirements Elaboration
(See 2.1.5 of **The Handbook**.*)*

> Produce an initial version of the requirements at the start of the project. Update and extend these requirements throughout the project.

Requirements Repository
(See 2.1.6 of **The Handbook**.*)*

> Make requirements and all elements that provide requirements-relevant information available through a repository.
> Treat the repository as one of the key resources of the project; keep it up to date.

Minimum Requirements Outcome

(See 2.1.7 of **The Handbook**.*)*

 This principle has been enforced in the Companion requirements case study (see Sect. 4.3).

> The requirements effort must always produce the following elements.
> For the Goals:
> - Key business objectives (**G.1**)
> - Key expected benefits (**G.3**)
> - Key stakeholders (**G.7**)
>
> For the System:
> - Key functions (**S.2**)
> - Overall division into clusters (**S.1**)

Appendix D: Principles and Good Practice Rules

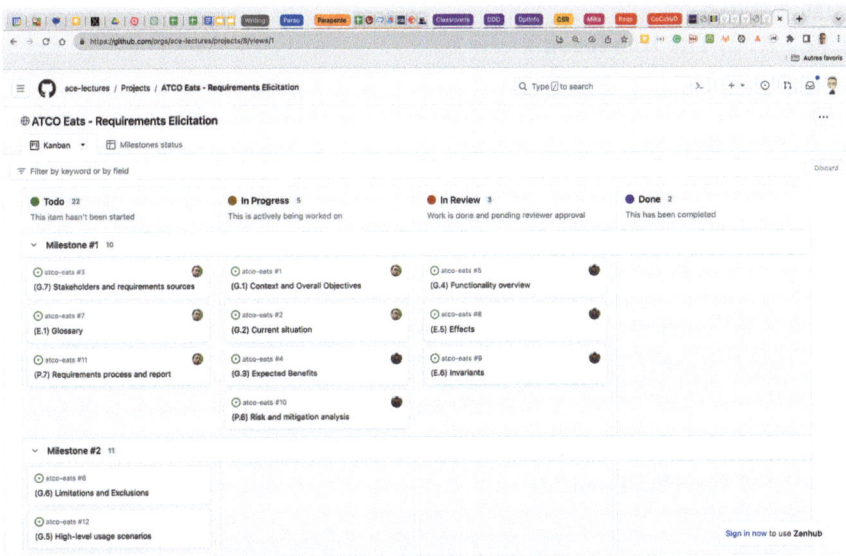

Fig. D.1 An illustration of a concrete completion of the standard plan (credit to McMaster University)

> For the Environment:
> - Key external constraints on the system (**E.3**)
>
> For the Project:
> - As essential guidance for the rest of the project: main milestones (**P.3**)
> - Also as part of this guidance: main **tasks** (**P.4**)

 The Handbook, in its 2022 edition, is mistakenly referencing P.5 instead of P.3.

 McMaster University has even defined a process to ensure the completion of the standard plan in its Requirements Engineering course CS/SE 3RA3[2] (see Fig. D.1).

User Acceptance Test
*(See 2.1.7 of **The Handbook**.)*

> Use the requirements as the basis for the User Acceptance Test plan.

Hence, every User Acceptance Test plan should refer specifically to at least one requirement.

---

[2] https://github.com/ace-lectures/cas-handbook-req-template

Stakeholders
(See 2.2.1 of **The Handbook.***)*

> Identify all stakeholders whose non-involvement might imperil the project; involve them.

Requirements Leadership
(See 2.2.2 of **The Handbook.***)*

> For all but small projects, requirements engineers (or business analysts) should lead the process of producing requirements.

Environment
(See 2.3 of **The Handbook.***)*

> Distinguish between system and environment properties.

Traceability
(See 2.4 of **The Handbook.***)*

> Throughout the project:
> - T1. Record all the consequences of the requirements for the project and system.
> - T2. Record the requirements sources of project and system elements.

Requirements Effort
(See 2.5 of **The Handbook.***)*

> Devote enough effort to guarantee requirements quality, but not so much as to detract from other tasks of the software development process.

For requirements, perfection is not the goal. The goal is good-enough quality, sufficient to obtain quality for the project and system as a whole without spending so much effort on the requirements as to detract from other tasks.

Requirements Abstraction
(See 4.7.2 of **The Handbook.***)*

> Express requirements without prejudice to design and implementation.

Appendix D: Principles and Good Practice Rules

Requirements Writing
(See 5.1 of **The Handbook**.*)*

> Start writing requirements as you gather them.

No-Synonym
(See 5.2.5 of **The Handbook**.*)*

> In requirements writing, enforce a one-to-one correspondence between important concepts (of the project, environment, goals, and system) and their names.

No-Repetition
(See 5.3 of **The Handbook**.*)*

> In requirements writing, never specify a **property** more than once.

This rule is sometimes known as "Single Point of Maintenance." In slogan form:

Say it well; say it once.

Reference
(See 5.3 of **The Handbook**.*)*

> Do not repeat: refer or refine.

Explanation
(See 5.4 of **The Handbook**.*)*

> - E1 In requirements, favor specifications over explanations.
> - E2 When explanatory elements are indispensable, devote special care to checking that they do not contradict the specification elements, even in small details.
> - E3 In requirements texts (and other forms of expression of requirements), use a clear and explicit convention to ensure that any explanatory elements stand out as distinct from specification elements.

Picture
(See 5.5.2 of **The Handbook.***)*

> Graphical illustrations in requirements texts must only use symbols—in particular those representing **components** and their connectors—with a precise semantics, defined in the illustrations themselves or in a common reference.
>
> Every pictorial variation must reflect a semantic variation.

Multiple Notation
(See 5.5.5 of **The Handbook.***)*

> In requirements using more than one notation, make sure that the binding specification of every **property** unambiguously appears in only one of notations.
>
> If elements in more than one notation pertain to a common property, make sure that the requirements clearly indicate which one is binding, and label the others as explanatory.

Identification
(See 5.7.4 of **The Handbook.***)*

> Every element appearing in requirements must have a **unique number or key** allowing unambiguous identification.

The numbering or the nomenclature of the key is a matter of internal policy. In the templates, we decided to use numbers and to restart from 1 in every chapter. This allows one to refer to a requirement with a clue about its kind. For example, in requirement G.1.1, G.1 refers to the chapter **G.1—Context and overall objectives**, and G.1.1 is the requirement number 1 in this chapter.

Glossary

(See 6.4 of **The Handbook.***)*

> Requirements must contain (in the Environment book) a list of all the domain-specific concepts relevant to the project and the corresponding definitions, endorsed by the respective qualified stakeholders.

 | In complement to the **Minimum Requirements Outcome Principle**, this chapter should not be empty.

Appendix D: Principles and Good Practice Rules

Acronym
(See 6.4.3 of **The Handbook.***)*

> In glossary entries introducing acronyms, do not just expand: explain.

Elicitation Coverage Principle
(See 6.10.2 of **The Handbook.***)*

> In soliciting requirements input from stakeholders, cover all four PEGS: Project, Environment, Goals, and System.

Feasibility Prototype
(See 6.11.5 of **The Handbook.***)*

> To avoid major project risks (**P.6**), the requirements effort should identify project-critical elements of needed technology (**P.5**), and in case of any doubt about their actual capabilities, develop and run feasibility prototypes to assess their readiness and adequacy for the project.

Prototype
(See 6.11.6 of **The Handbook.***)*

> When used with the appropriate caution, prototypes are an important tool in the requirements elicitation process.
> Distinguish requirements prototypes from incremental system versions obtained in iterative development.
> Always present a requirements prototype as such, identifying the system properties that it is intended to assess and avoiding any confusion with the actual system and any misplaced expectation.

Risk
(See 6.11.7 of **The Handbook.***)*

> The analysis of any identified risk (particularly in **P.6—Risks and Mitigation Analysis**) must include the following elements:
> - R1. Identification of the risk
> - R2. Assessment of the likelihood that it will materialize
> - R3. Assessment of the damage to the project (cost, delays, etc.)
> - R4. Description of the mitigation strategy or strategies, if any
> - R5. Assessment of the cost of the retained mitigation strategy or strategies, if any

Scenario
(See 7.6 of **The Handbook**.*)*

> Take advantage of use cases, user stories, use case slices, tests, and other forms of scenarios as tools for elicitation and verification of requirements. Do not use them as a substitute for actual requirements specifications.

Document Completeness
(See 11.1 of **The Handbook**.*)*

> A set of requirements is **document-complete** if it includes all expected elements:
> 1. If the requirements are devised to follow a template, such as the PEGS plan or IEEE-830, all parts required by the template.
> 2. Appropriate front matter including names of authors and endorsers, table of contents, and any other needed meta-information as may be required by organizational standards, such as a table of figures, a bibliography, and an index.
> 3. Proper numbering of all elements such as paragraphs and figures, with a unique identification of every element, allowing it to be referenced unambiguously.
> 4. All figures and formal elements announced in texts.
> 5. Up-to-date values for all cross-references between requirements elements.
> 6. The precise references to all other documents, such as articles from the technical literature or industry standards, cited in or used by the requirements.
> 7. If any TBDs ("To Be Determined") remain, application of the TBD rule, including the presence of a TBD list.

Goal Completeness
(See 11.2 of **The Handbook**.*)*

> A set of requirements is **goal-complete** if for every goal there exist project or system requirements ensuring the achievement of that goal.

Make sure that the project members are aware of the Goals book, particularly **G.3**, and regularly consult it. The project should pay constant attention to goals, and update them when new circumstances lead to departures from the original project focus. To assess goal completeness, check that project documents, in particular in the System book, as well as design elements and code, refer to the Goals and remain consistent with them.

 | This implies a strong traceability mechanism.

Scenario Completeness
(See 11.3 of **The Handbook***.)*

> A set of requirements is **scenario-complete** if for every identified scenario the specification of functionality includes enough information to support the scenario.

For this, check every step of the scenarios (**G.5** and **S.4**) to ensure that there is enough specification elsewhere (particularly **S.2**) to realize it.

Environment Completeness
(See 11.4 of **The Handbook***.)*

> A set of requirements for a system is **environment-complete** if it identifies, as part of the environment's specification, all constraints, assumptions, effects, and invariants relevant to the system.

The four elements (constraints, assumptions, effects, and invariants) correspond to, respectively, the **E.3**, **E.4**, **E.5**, and **E.6** chapters of the Environment book.

Here are some guidelines to ensuring and assessing environment completeness:

- Systematically examine the results of stakeholder interviews and workshops (**P.7**) for properties of the environment that might have been missed.
- Perform a similar check on other requirements sources such as meeting minutes and legal contracts (see "Preparatory discussions" of **The Handbook**).
- Check that environment properties are characterized as such and appear in the Environment book.

Interface Completeness
(See 11.5 of **The Handbook***.)*

> A set of requirements for a system is **interface-complete** if it identifies all required technology elements and all the interfaces it will offer to other systems.

This concerns both interfaces:

- Expected from the environment and described mainly in **P.5—Required Technology Elements**
- Provided to the environment (user interfaces, APIs), mainly described in **S3—Interfaces**

Command-Query Completeness
(See 11.6 of **The Handbook.***)*

> Ensure, and check, that the System requirements make it possible to determine, after the application of any Creator and Command on any object, the value of any Query applicable to the object.

The principle comes from the classical Abstract Data Types observations that operations on the objects of a system belong to three categories:

- Queries, which return information about objects
- Commands, which modify objects
- Creators (or "constructors"), which initialize objects

Not-All-Sprints-Are-Created-Equal ("NASACE")
(See 12.7.2 of **The Handbook.***)*

> 1. Every sprint includes a definition phase and an implementation phase.
> 2. Both of these phases involve verification.
> 3. Definition dominates early sprints and decreases afterward.
> 4. Implementation starts on a small scale with the earliest sprints and increases afterward.
> 5. Verification becomes dominant in the latest sprints.

This contradicts the classical agile view of a single scheme for all sprints but integrates **RUP** and Waterfall ideas that are closer to real-life projects.

Appendix E: Book Templates

▼ ⊘ *Corresponding Requirement*

This section satisfies requirements **G3.1** and **S.1.1.3** (see Sect. 5.2).

We provide a set of Book templates to help the reader apply PEGS and organize your requirements, all available in the **companion website**. Here is the list of the available templates (feel free to contribute by submitting to the authors additional templates):

 Some content of the templates (e.g., the change log table) needs to be removed or adapted. We have recalled what kind of material each chapter should contain. In some sections, we provide examples of information that should not be there. We do not aim to be exhaustive. These examples come from classical errors we have identified from initial teaching usages we have experienced.

DOCX
Word being one of the most used text editor, we provide a template for its user.

Google Doc
A more useful template as using references and links are more natural in that format.

AsciiDoc
Our recommended format (used to write most of our case studies, including this whole **companion book**). **AsciiDoc** is a popular format for online documentation. ○ **GitHub** pages natively support it, for example. As a plain textual format (separating content from rendering), it allows tools to process it, as illustrated in some of our quality rules implementations.

 McMaster University has adapted the template to their Requirements Engineering course **CS/SE 3RA3**.

LaTeX

LaTeX is a popular text editor, highly used in academia, with the same benefits as **AsciiDoc**, but which requires more tooling.

We are currently working on additional templates that might be available by the time of publishing (stay tuned at the **companion website**), e.g., **Jira Software** (an application life cycle management solution for software development teams), **SysML** (a systems engineering modeling language that supports requirements definition and traceability), **Polarion** (a popular requirements engineering tool that supports dynamic documentation generation).

GitHub

As detailed in Sect. 4.4, the GitHub template we are providing in the **companion website** (available directly at https://github.com/FormalRequirements/HandBookTemplate/) contains ways to directly express requirements as issues.

Thanks to the notion of `Project`, where issues can be sorted, listed, and organized, our **GitHub** template provides a ready-to-use project organized in chapters following the standard plan (see Fig. 4.11).

Antora

A static Web site generator, based on **AsciiDoc**. It allows very nice Web site generation (see Fig. E.1) and is available as a **GitHub** repository you can freely clone from the **companion website**.

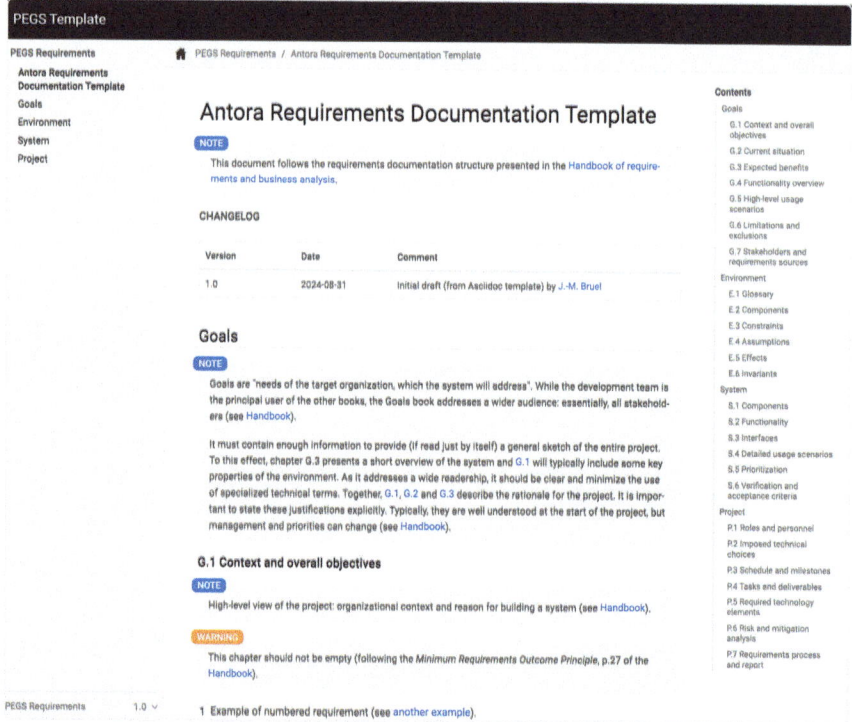

Fig. E.1 The Antora template

Appendix F: 🎓 Exercises: Elements of Solutions

In the following sections, if an element of solution corresponds to an exercise in **The Handbook**, it is referenced by its number in the book. Otherwise, it is numbered with an `extra` prefix. The icon on the left of the solution indicates, whether:

- It has been validated by Bertrand Meyer.
- It has not been validated by Bertrand Meyer.
- It is a wrong answer (for quiz purposes or simply as an example of common mistake).

F.1. Requirements: Basic Concepts and Definitions

1-E.1 Silence and noise
A document prepared by Bettina Bair for a requirements course **Bair 2005** presents a sample requirements document covering a Web-based sales system for a fictitious company. Imagine you are in the team tasked with implementing these requirements. Relying on your informal understanding of the problem domain, identify any cases of silence and noise in this document.

	Sections' number taken from the corresponding list of requirements in Bair 2005
	The end of the exercise "identify any cases of (A) silence (B) in this document" should be "identify any cases of (A) silence and (B) noise in this document."

Silences
  Here is a non-exhaustive list:
  - The notion of *training* is only mentioned in 3.2. What does "x days of training mean" (consecutive days, every year, etc.)?
  - In the use case *Request Assistance* (end of section 5), it is said "[the customer]… has previously been assisted by a sales agent, that same agent is selected." But what happens if this sales agent is not in the company anymore?

Noises
  Here is a non-exhaustive list:
  - The glossary (Appendix 7) is not a requirement and should be in a separate document (Environment book E1).

1-E.3   Constraints and assumptions
Give more examples of **constraints** and **assumption**, from application domains of your choice. Explain your rationale for classifying each example as a constraint or an assumption.
Solution
Here is a non-exhaustive list:
- Constraints
    - The companion book should itself apply the method described in the Handbook. *(As it makes the life of the authors harder)*
- Assumptions
    - The companion book will be reviewed by the author of the Handbook. *(As it makes the life of the authors easier)*

F.2.   Requirements: General Principles

2-E.1
The Requirements Elaboration Principle (see **here**) states that a successful requirements process results from a trade-off between two extremes: requirements-upfront-only (Waterfall style) and requirements-only-as-you-go (agile style). Can you think of specific project types or circumstances in which the trade-off should be strongly tilted toward one of these extreme variants? Give examples for both, and explain the rationale for your assessment.
Solution
Here are some examples:
- The refactoring of a legacy system (let's say a Flight company reservation system), to only change the programming language but none of its functionalities (example of Waterfall style). One reason might be to save from changing final user habits.
- The brand new software of a brand-new start-up, with a very dynamic market (example of agile style). The rationale is clearly that the company requires their software to always be upfront of the concurrent ones.

2-E.2
A dating site is updating its software. Who are the stakeholders? (See the Stakeholders Principle **here**.)
Solution
Here are some possible stakeholders:
- Individuals (looking for a date)
- Publicity companies (to place advertisements)
- Couple/Sex/Psy/Consulting companies (to advertise their business)
- Bar/Events companies (to advertise dating-related events)
- RGPD and lawyers (to check that privacy concerns are respected)

Appendix F: Exercises: Elements of Solutions 159

2-E.3
In line with the Requirements Effort Principle (see **here**), give examples (either abstract or based on your project experience) of cases in which it is necessary or at least legitimate to sacrifice requirements quality for the greater benefit of the final system's quality. Explain the rationale. To specify the aspects of requirements quality being sacrificed, you may refer to the analysis of requirements quality factors in chapter 4 of **The Handbook**.

The Handbook, in its 2022 edition, is mistakenly referencing section 2.2.1 instead of section 2.5 for Requirements Quality.

Solution
The requirements for this companion book (see Sect. 5.2) constitute a perfect illustration. We have not looked for absolute quality, but we pragmatically write what could help getting the best result possible.

F.3. Standard Plan for Requirements

3-E.1 Finding the right place
State the chapter from the standard plan (such as P.1) to which each one of the following example requirements would belong:
1. Some of the general constraints were defined in the preliminary meeting of June 15, 2022, available at [URL].
2. The login record shall be implemented using MongoDB.
3. Here is the basic scheme of interaction for ordering a product: [followed by the description of that scheme].
4. The project shall only use external software products available through an approved open-source license (GPL or Creative Commons).
5. The product shall be available on mobile platforms as well as through an API.
6. Any use of cookies shall conform to the GDPR.
7. As a result of the introduction of the new payroll system, pay periods shall be standardized to monthly for all employees.
8. As the system depends on Windows 11 facilities, meeting the schedule depends on Microsoft fully releasing Windows 11 by the end of October 2021.
9. This function is considered critical to the deployment of the project.
10. Upon exiting a session, the system shall memorize the last explored directory as the restart point for the next session.

Solution
As advised in Sect. 2.1.4, let us first find the corresponding books.

Req #	Book	Explanations
1	Goal	Origin/Source of the requirements
2	Project	A technical constraint
3	Goal	A high-level scenario (system if considered low level)
4	Project	Constraint on the project
5	System	Technical details
6	Environ.	Constraint from the environment
7	Environ.	An effect on the environment (could be Goal if considered as a high-level objective)

#		Explanations
8	Project	Describes a risk
9	System	Describes a priority between system's functions
10	System	A behavior

Note that some words can be misleading. For example, "Some of the general constraints were defined in…" can be intuitively attached to the Environment book, because of the word "constraint." But in fact, here, the statement is about the source; hence, it could be a dependency for a high-level goal. This is why, in this particular example, it belongs to the **G7—Stakeholders and Requirements Sources** chapter. Now we can refine the table in a second step and be more precise.

#	Ch.	Explanations
1	G.7	Reference source about the origin of the constraints (may be recalled in E.3)
2	P.2	An imposed technical choice
3	G.5	High-level scenario (could be S.4 if considered low level)
4	P.2	Imposed technical choices on the project
5	S.3	Technical details about interfacing
6	E.3	Constraint from the environment
7	E.5	Describes an effect (can be an considered as an expected benefit in G.3)
8	P.6	Describes a risk
9	S.5	Describes a priority between system's functions
10	S.2	A behavior (may also appear in a scenario in S.4)

 If you cannot identify a particular chapter in the book identified in first step, this might mean that you have picked up the wrong book for this requirement.

For question 8, if the sentence would have been "The system depends on Windows 11 facilities," it would have been P.5. But the requirement here is about the risk related to the release date (hence P.6). In the preparation of this companion book, we had discussions about the difference between an expected benefits and an effect (see, e.g., requirement 7). These discussions are reflected in Section B.1.10.

> Having a debate between stakeholders for the place of a particular requirement in the standard plan is exactly the expected benefit: a clarification about this particular requirement, which might lead to a reformulation, the addition of a precision, etc.

F.4. Complementary Exercises

F.4.1. Object-Oriented Requirements

1. In the following code, find the invariants error:

```eiffel
class INSURANCE_CLAIM feature
    -- Boolean queries (all with default value False):
  is_investigated, is_evaluated, is_reserved, is_agreed,
  is_imposed, is_resolved: BOOLEAN
  investigate
    -- Conduct investigation on validity of claim. Set is_investigated.
    deferred
    ensure
      is_investigated
    end
  evaluate
      -- Assess monetary amount of damages.
    require
      is_investigated
    deferred
    ensure
      is_evaluated
      -- Note: is_investigated still holds (see the invariant at the end of the class text).
    end
  set_reserve
      -- Assess monetary amount of damages. Set is_reserved.
    require
      is_investigated
      -- Note: we do not require is_evaluated.
    deferred
    ensure
      is_reserved
    end
  negotiate
      -- Assess monetary amount of damages. Set is_agreed only if negotiation
      -- leads to an agreement with the claim originator.
    require
      is_reserved
      is_evaluated
    deferred
    ensure
      is_reserved
      -- See the invariant for is_evaluated and is_investigated.
    end
  impose (amount: INTEGER)
      -- Determine amount of claim if negotiation fails. Set is_imposed.
    require
      not is_agreed is_reserved
    deferred
```

```
44         ensure
45            is_imposed
46         end
47    resolve
48            -- Finalize handling of claim. Set is_resolved.
49         require
50            is_agreed or is_imposed
51         deferred
52         require
53            is_resolved
54         end
55 invariant  -- ⟦⇒⟧ is logical implication.
56            is_evaluated => is_investigated
57            is_reserved  => is_evaluated
58            is_resolved  => is_agreed or is_imposed
59            is_agreed    => is_evaluated
60            is_imposed   => is_evaluated
61            is_imposed   => not is_agreed  -- Hence, by laws of logic,
      is_agreed => not is_imposed
62 end
```

Solution

Error is in line 57. The class invariant includes is_reserved ⇒ is_evaluated, while set_reserve requires only is_investigated, and actually makes an explicit note that is_evaluated is not required. The class invariant was intended to instead read is_reserved ⇒ is_investigated.

F.4.2. The Standard Plan

1. According to your understanding of the four books, try to define a dependability graph where, for each book, you draw dependability lines with the books they might depend on (talk about).
  ▼ *Solution*
  See Fig. 2.23.
2. Where (in which book's chapter) would you place the following requirements:

Requirement	chapter #
The system should support plane ticket booking.	
The account administrator can upgrade the withdrawal limit of the owner's credit card.	
The development of the application will follow the Scrum agile method.	

Requirement	chapter #
The system should support plane ticket booking.	S.2

Appendix F: Exercises: Elements of Solutions

Requirement	chapter #
The account administrator can upgrade the withdrawal limit of the owner's credit card.	P.1
The development of the application will follow the Scrum agile method.	P.2

1. State the chapter from the standard plan (such as P.1) to which each one of the following example requirements would belong:
   (a) The project shall produce a first release by October 31, 2023.
   (b) All Web sites shall conform to GDPR (EU privacy rules).
   (c) The Bridge Maintenance System shall limit bridge closures to no more than one night a month.
   (d) After five failed login attempts, access shall be blocked for 30 min.

▼ *Solution*

Req #	Chapter	Explanations
1	P.3	Clearly a milestone
2	E.3	Legal constraint
3	G.3	High-level objective (can be an considered as an effect in E.5.)
4	S.2	A functional feature

F.4.3. Requirements Category

1. For the following list of (unrelated) requirements, find their category:
   (a) The input-output system ensures that the temperature value originally entered by the user, if validated, is in the allowable range of −20 to +40 °C.
   (b) Increase by 20% the proportion of graduates finding suitable jobs 6 months or less after completing their studies. *(For a system matching university graduates with job offers)*
   (c) The current manual operation of trains requires a minimum interval of 2 min between successive trains, preventing the tracks from operating at full capacity and making it impossible to meet the expected growth of traffic over the next 10 years. *(For a system devised to automate train operation and increase train frequency)*
   (d) For past auctions, the hammer price shall be displayed only to registered users. *(For an auction Web site)*
   (e) Any purchase over EUR 5000 requires two authorized signatures. *(For a bank transfer system)*
   (f) All pilots can understand messages in basic English. *(For a flight control system)*
   (g) Safety regulations for aircraft are as defined by IATA.
   (h) The network can only guarantee a minimum bandwidth of 1 Mbit/s. *(In a software system relying on a network)*
   (i) The available bandwidth will be 1 Mbit/s or more. *(In a software system*

relying on a network)

(j) Running the payroll system will cause transfers to the bank accounts that employees have registered with the company. *(For a payment system)*

(k) When the system is put into operation, employees will be paid on the last working day of the month (whatever the practice was before). *(For a payment system)*

(l) The system expects a temperature between 18 and 25 °C (precondition) and maintains it in that range (postcondition). *(For a factory control system, including two sensors to measure the temperature and air-conditioning units to control it)*

(m) UI development shall be the responsibility of the Bangalore division.

(n) The "Justify" command applied to a paragraph shall result in all its lines having an equal number of characters. *(In a text-processing system)*

(o) The lead-tracking system shall be designed for use by marketing reps.

(p) Operation of the system for 24/7 availability shall be the responsibility of the central IT group.

(q) Networking protocols appear in section S.3.X.

(r) The maximum allowed time of 100 ms for this input operation is necessary to meet the goal of immediate user feedback discussed in section G.4.X.

(s) The director is not consistent in his decision-making.

(t) The presence of two signature fields follows from the rule on purchases higher than € 5000 (section E.3.X).

▼ *Solution*

Req #	Category
1	Responsibility (System book)
2	Goal (Goal book)
3	Obstacle (Goal book)
4	Constraint (Environment book)
5	Business rule (Environment book)
6	Assumption (Environment book)
7	Role (Environment book)
8	Constraint (Environment book)
9	Assumption (Environment book)
10	Functional (System book)
11	Effect (Goal book)
12	Invariant (Environment book)
13	Role (Project book)
14	(Functional) Behavior (System book)
15	Role (Goal book)
16	Role (System book)
17	Meta
18	Justification
19	Noise
20	Justification

Appendix G: Handbook Errors in the First Edition (2022)

Between the first edition of **The Handbook** and the edition of this **companion book**, several typos and errors have been discovered there. We list here the ones found during the writing of this **companion book**.

- p.18: The end of Exercise 1-E.1, "Identify any cases of (A) silence (B) in this document," should be "Identify any cases of (A) silence and (B) noise in this document."
- p.27: The Minimum Requirements Outcome Principle is mistakenly referencing P.5 instead of P.3 for the milestones.
- p.33: Exercise 3-E.3 is mistakenly referencing section 2.2.1 instead of the 2.5 one, for Requirements Quality. It also refers to the "Requirements Quality Principle" but means in fact "Requirements Effort Principle."
- p.47: In the table, the `Delimited` attribute is mentioned as applying to all, but in definition p.69, it applies only to Goal and System. So `all` should be replaced by `Goal, System`.
- p.158: "May refer to Goal, System and Environment classes." (System is missing.)
- p.165, `r in, then the power of...` should be `r in AxA, then the power of...`

References and Links

- Ian Sommerville and Pete Sawyer, Requirements Engineering: A Good Practice Guide. Wiley. 2004.
- Axel van Lamsweerde: Requirements Engineering, From System Goals to UML Models to Software Specifications. Wiley. https://www.info.ucl.ac.be/~avl/book.php
- Klaus Pohl: Requirements Engineering Fundamentals, Principles, and Techniques. Textbook, Jan 2025. https://link.springer.com/book/9783662692042.
- Karl Wiegers, Joy Beatty: Software Requirements, 3rd Edition. Microsoft Press. 2013.
- M. Jackson and P. Zave, "Domain Descriptions," Proceedings of the IEEE International Symposium on Requirements Engineering, 1992.
- Jean-Michel Bruel, Raphael Faudou: An Industrial Feedback on Model-Based Requirements Engineering in Systems Engineering Context. MODRE Workshop at MODELS. 2016.
- ISO/IEC/IEEE 29148:2018 Systems and software engineering—Life cycle processes—Requirements engineering. https://www.iso.org/obp/ui/#iso:std:iso-iec-ieee:29148:ed-2:v1:en.
- **The Handbook** website: https://se.ethz.ch/requirements.
- The *Streamlining Workforce Management* real-life case study: https://library.constructor.org/node/97.
- Jean-Michel Bruel, Sophie Ebersold, Florian Galinier, Manuel Mazzara, Alexandr Naumchev, Bertrand Meyer: The Role of Formalism in System Requirements. ACM Computing Survey 54(5): 93:1–93:36 (2022). https://dblp.org/rec/journals/csur/BruelEGMNM21.

We list in the following the links that appear **like that** in the electronic version of this **companion book**.

Word	URL
AsciiDoc	https://asciidoc.org/
Bertrand Meyer	https://bertrandmeyer.com/
Bertrand Meyer's Handbook (on Springerlink)	https://link.springer.com/content/pdf/10.1007/978-3-031-06739-6.pdf
BON	https://en.wikipedia.org/wiki/Business_Object_Notation
CESAMES	http://cesames.cn/wp-content/uploads/2020/06/CESAM-Systems-Architecting-Method-Pocket-Guide-CESAMES.pdf
ChatGPT	https://chatgpt.com/
companion website	https://requirements.university/
Constructor University	https://constructor.university/
Cucumber	https://cucumber.io/
GitHub	https://github.com
Jira	https://www.atlassian.com/fr/software/jira
J.-M. Bruel	https://jmbruel.netlify.app
Mariya Naumcheva	https://www.linkedin.com/in/mnaumcheva/
McMaster University	https://www.mcmaster.ca/
Polarion	https://polarion.plm.automation.siemens.com/products/polarion-requirements
Sophie Ebersold	https://www.irit.fr/~Sophie.Ebersold
SysML	https://www.omgsysml.org/

MIX
Papier aus verantwortungsvollen Quellen
Paper from responsible sources
FSC® C105338

If you have any concerns about our products,
you can contact us on
ProductSafety@springernature.com

In case Publisher is established outside the EU,
the EU authorized representative is:
**Springer Nature Customer Service Center GmbH
Europaplatz 3, 69115 Heidelberg, Germany**

Printed by Libri Plureos GmbH
in Hamburg, Germany